T0318328

# CHRISTIAN ETHICS

*Christian Ethics: The Basics* sets out clearly and critically the different ways that Augustine, Aquinas and Luther continue to shape ethics today within and across Christian denominations. It assumes no previous knowledge of the subject and can be read by religious believers and non-believers alike. Readers are introduced to Christian ethics from the ground up before being invited to consider some of the most controversial but important questions facing people across the world today.

Topics addressed include:

- Social justice
- War and peace
- Migration/immigration
- Climate change
- Euthanasia
- Same-sex marriage
- Religiously-inspired violence
- Biotechnology
- Abrahamic ethics

Concise, readable and authoritative, this is the ideal primer for anyone interested in the study of religious ethics and Christianity.

**Robin Gill** is Emeritus Professor of Applied Theology at the University of Kent. He is the author or editor of 40 books, including *Moral Passion and Christian Ethics* (2017), *A Textbook of Christian Ethics* (4th ed., 2014) and *Sociological Theology* (3 vols., 2012).

# THE BASICS

For more information about this series, please visit: https://www.routledge.com/The-Basics/book-series/B

# CHRISTIAN ETHICS

# **THE BASICS**

**ROBIN GILL**

Routledge
Taylor & Francis Group

LONDON AND NEW YORK

First published 2020
by Routledge
2 Park Square, Milton Park, Abingdon, Oxon OX14 4RN

and by Routledge
52 Vanderbilt Avenue, New York, NY 10017

*Routledge is an imprint of the Taylor & Francis Group, an informa business*

*British Library Cataloguing-in-Publication Data*
A catalogue record for this book is available from the British Library

*Library of Congress Cataloging-in-Publication Data*
Names: Gill, Robin, author.
Title: Christian ethics : the basics / Robin Gill.
Description: Abingdon, Oxon ; New York, NY : Routledge, 2020. |
Includes bibliographical references and index.
Identifiers: LCCN 2019051038 (print) | LCCN 2019051039 (ebook) |
ISBN 9780367331108 (hardback) | ISBN 9780367331092 (paperback) |
ISBN 9780429318030 (ebook)
Subjects: LCSH: Christian ethics.
Classification: LCC BJ1261 .G55 2020 (print) | LCC BJ1261 (ebook) |
DDC 241--dc23
LC record available at https://lccn.loc.gov/2019051038
LC ebook record available at https://lccn.loc.gov/2019051039

ISBN: 978-0-367-33110-8 (hbk)
ISBN: 978-0-367-33109-2 (pbk)
ISBN: 978-0-429-31803-0 (ebk)

Typeset in Bembo
by Taylor & Francis Books

# CONTENTS

# ACKNOWLEDGEMENTS

All the quotations from the Bible in this book come from the well-respected NRSV.

I am most grateful to all the people who have helped me with this short introduction to Christian ethics. Academic colleagues and generations of students at Edinburgh, Newcastle and, finally, Kent Universities helped me with successive editions of my *A Textbook of Christian Ethics*. Five anonymous reviewers for Routledge offered valuable criticisms of my draft proposal for this present book, and then my son Martin Gill, my friend and former colleague Dr Alan Le Grys, and another anonymous Routledge reviewer read through the first full draft of its text and offered a number of crucial, and always helpful, points for revision. Few of us can spot all our own errors and shortcomings. We need our colleagues to do that. Thank you so much to all of them: their help has been invaluable. Remaining stupidities are, of course, entirely my own.

Robin Gill
4 October 2019
The Festival of St Francis of Assisi

# INTRODUCTION

The discipline of Christian ethics raises important questions – some large and others small but complex. This book presumes no prior knowledge of the discipline and it will not give a definitive answer to all the questions it raises.

It also makes no presuppositions about where you are coming from. You might be a Christian belonging to a specific denomination or an unattached Christian. Or you might, say, be Jewish, Muslim or Buddhist. Or you might see yourself as agnostic, as wholly secular, or as a committed atheist. And you might be reading this book to understand your own faith a bit better or you might simply be reading it out of curiosity.

Does this matter? Well it may indeed matter to you (as it does to me) but this short introduction to the discipline has been designed to be read by people coming from a wide range of different perspectives. Its aim is to bring some clarity to the questions raised by any serious attempt to study the different ways that Christian ethics is, and has been, articulated across time and across different global cultures.

Why is that important? One answer is simply this: the values variously held by Christians have long shaped Western culture and have spread widely into, say, Africa, Australasia and Melanesia, and even into parts of Asia and the Far East. Any serious attempt to understand global culture would be deficient if it ignored the various and complex ways that these values have been generated. Understanding something about the history of Christian ethics, and the ongoing tensions within Christian ethics today, is simply part of being properly educated.

There is another important reason: even though many European, Australasian and some North American churches have experienced declining and aging congregations over the last two generations, religious tensions in the West and elsewhere have considerably increased. Following the attack upon the Twin Towers in New York in 2001, religiously inspired violence seems to have increased around the world. Before that shocking event there was Catholic/Protestant sectarian violence in Northern Ireland in the 1960s and a rise in Islamic militancy in the Middle East since the late 1970s. More recently there have been right-wing anti-Islamic extremist attacks in Norway, New Zealand and elsewhere – some apparently motivated by their perpetrators' understanding of Christianity.

One response to this violence has been to argue that, as religious belonging declines, so will the violence. However, at most that can be only a partial 'solution'. It is not clear that religious belonging is declining at a global level and, even within Europe, it is attendances at churches and synagogues, rather than mosques, that are currently declining.

A more effective response to religiously inspired violence might be to encourage people of different faiths (secular as well as religious) to study their faiths more carefully and critically in a global context. Viewed in this way, a serious study of Christian ethics in all of its complexity – with its varying strengths, weaknesses and opportunities – might contribute to a less fractious global religious culture and, even, to a more peaceful world.

## HOW TO USE THIS BOOK

This book is written as a starter-pack or taster. The chapters that follow can be read in any order. They are designed to be fairly self-contained, with plenty of cross-references. The case-studies at the end of Chapters 2–7 can also be read in isolation

For those wishing to study Christian ethics at greater depth, suggestions are made at the end of every chapter. The first four chapters correspond exactly to the first four sections of my *A Textbook of Christian Ethics: Fourth Edition* (London, New Delhi, New York and Sydney: Bloomsbury, 2014). This is quite a lengthy textbook designed to be used by second-year university students. As will be indicated in the **further reading** at the end of each chapter, many of the quotations in this book can be found at much greater length in the *Textbook*. This is a deliberate policy as it allows a secure bridge to this level of further study.

The next level, to final honours or postgraduate standard, suggested in the further reading is to a series of monographs that I edit for Cambridge University Press: **New Studies in Christian Ethics**. There are now some 40 single-author books in this ongoing series dating back to 1992, with the most recent listed at the end of this Introduction. The two key aims of this series are: to promote monographs in Christian ethics which engage centrally with the present secular ethical debate at the highest possible intellectual level; and to encourage contributors to demonstrate that Christian ethics can make a distinctive contribution to this debate. So be warned, these monographs are not for the faint-hearted. However, many of them have had outstanding reviews from other academics.

In the first chapter of one of my own contributions to this series, **Moral Passion and Christian Ethics** (2017), I offer a critical overview of all the books published up to that point in *New Studies in Christian Ethics*. Reading this chapter carefully could be another way of progressing to this demanding level of Christian ethics.

At whatever level you take your study of Christian ethics, my hope is that you enjoy it as much as I do. It is a fascinating, albeit complex, subject.

## ETHICS OR MORALS?

Some people make a sharp distinction between ethics and morals. Ethics is often seen as an academic study of ideas and theories. In contrast, morals are seen as being concerned with how people actually behave in relation to each other. On this understanding we can debate rationally with other people about, say, some difficult, even speculative, ethical choices; for example, about whether it would ever be ethical to clone human beings or edit their genes. However, daily living also requires us to be moral human beings, behaving properly towards other people. In that sense, ethics is an intellectual activity, whereas morals are about proper behaviour to others.

Unfortunately this neat distinction soon breaks down. We do talk about both ethical behaviour and moral behaviour. We also talk about ethical theory and moral theory. Among academics we also use both the term 'Christian ethics' and the term 'moral theology'.

Doubtless this debate will continue. Academics who insist upon a difference between 'Christian ethics' and 'moral theology' often view the latter as being more *theological*. That is to say it is theological or doctrinal considerations that are central to the discipline. I will return to that point in a moment.

However, simply in terms of derivation, the word 'ethics' comes from Greek and the word 'morals' from Latin. In both it tends to mean 'customs' ... itself not a very satisfactory understanding in a world faced with serious, even life-threatening, ethical/moral choices. For clarity this book will for the most part use the term 'Christian ethics'.

## STYLES OF ETHICAL ARGUMENT

Another point that will be assumed in this book is that, when describing ethical theories, there are common features that can be found in both secular and Christian forms of ethics (or, indeed, in Islamic ethics, Buddhist ethics or ethics of other faith traditions). In very broad terms, four styles of argument are particularly relevant to ethical decision-making (whether they are religiously based or not): arguments based upon principles; arguments based upon consequences; arguments based upon personal situations; and arguments based upon virtue or character.

These styles are not always mutually exclusive and regularly occur alongside each other in public debates. However, in academic terms they are distinct and each has its own literature.

### ARGUMENTS BASED UPON PRINCIPLES

The language of human rights is a clear expression of this style of ethical argument. Once a particular human right is accepted as binding then one cannot argue beyond it. Of course, it may conflict with another binding human right and that is likely to lead to considerable debate. Yet that debate will not be about whether a particular right is itself binding but about how it can be implemented in relation to another binding right.

So, most people today would agree that slavery is simply wrong and that all people have a right not to be enslaved. Sadly slavery does still exist in the world, but most of us conclude that it is still wrong. We are aware, of course, that slavery in the past was not always thought to be wrong. However, today there is broad agreement that our ancestors were in error about this and that slavery is and always was wrong.

Again, we can debate about whether some instance of apparent slavery today really is slavery. Is, for example, an immigrant working illegally but voluntarily in California or Europe for payment well below a minimum national wage to be regarded as a 'slave'? Some people might say so, but much depends here upon the word 'voluntarily'.

Or, to take the emerging issues of human reproductive cloning and editing human genes, an ethical argument based upon a principle might maintain that they are wrong because they are against nature. Within nature a baby needs both a mother and a father to be born and is born with fixed genes. A person born using reproductive cloning would have the DNA of a single individual (including the mitochondria if that individual were female). A baby born after gene editing would have a pattern of genes different from that inherited from her or his parents. In neither case could this happen in nature.

## ARGUMENTS BASED UPON CONSEQUENCES

In contrast to the language of rights or principles, the focus of these arguments is upon the consequences or effects of a particular ethical choice. Are the consequences or effects of a particular choice desirable or appropriate? For instance, do they contribute to human happiness?

To return to slavery, many of the arguments used to justify it in the 18th century were based upon the dire economic consequences of abolishing slavery. Huge wealth in Britain generated from plantations in the West Indies depended heavily upon slave labour. People back in Britain would suffer economic hardship without this wealth, so it was argued, and slaves themselves would face an uncertain future outside these plantations. In short, many people would be unhappy without slavery and, in the southern states of America for instance, households would be unable to cope without their domestic slaves.

In the 21st century, of course, these arguments based upon consequences can (with hindsight) be readily reversed. After all, the abolition of the slave trade did not inevitably lead to these dire consequences for the British people, for American households in the deep south, or for slaves themselves. Arguably, the overall consequences of abolition actually proved to be beneficial in the long-term.

Again, with human reproductive cloning or gene editing, the ethical argument against them from this perspective might be that they are wrong because they involve the possibility of serious risks. Consider, for instance, the cloning of pets and farm animals: for any successes there are many failures. Similarly with the gene editing of plants or animals. Perhaps (or perhaps not) such consequences are acceptable for plants or even animals, but many might regard them as thoroughly unacceptable for human beings – especially since these new techniques might involve unknown risks to future generations.

Or, to reverse the argument, ethicists who defend the possibility of either technique usually do so because they offer the possibility of eliminating serious diseases from vulnerable families. In short, they are justified for their potentially beneficial health consequences.

## ARGUMENTS BASED UPON PERSONAL SITUATIONS

This style of ethical argument typically denies that there are any binding rights or principles, and appeals instead to individual feelings, conscience or love (rather than to impersonal consequences). In a particular situation, what is the most loving thing to do?

Perhaps in the 18th century some householders with an elderly loyal slave did believe that retaining their slave really was the most loving thing to do *for her*. In the 21st century, of course, we realise that treating someone as a slave is not the most loving thing to do in our situation today. The rightness or wrongness of slavery, so it is maintained here, depends entirely upon context.

Similarly with human reproductive cloning or gene editing: on this approach, we should consider each case as it comes, asking whether or not it is the most loving thing to do. That is exactly what pet-owners do when they ask for their favourite dog or cat to be cloned. They loved the first pet so much that they want to reproduce it as nearly as possible. The cloned pet would then be loved just as much as the original pet was loved. Would it be wrong, some ask, to extend this argument to much-loved humans?

### ARGUMENTS BASED UPON VIRTUES OR CHARACTER

This style of ethical argument has points in common with the previous one but a rather different focus. It typically starts not from a tricky ethical dilemma but from a discussion of the ethical character of the person or community that is doing the arguing. It is less concerned with the question 'Is a particular action right?' than with the question 'Are we acting virtuously?'

So, in the context of 18th century slavery, the question becomes 'Is a slave-owning society really virtuous?' Most people today would answer with a resounding 'no' to that question. We look back with horror to that aspect of the 18th century and are shocked that slave-owners then could consider themselves to be virtuous.

Some people today react similarly to the possibility of human reproductive cloning or gene editing. They regard this possibility as yet another example of the 'commodification' of human life. Alternatively, others might consider that such human ingenuity and creativity is actually virtuous, especially when it aims to eliminate harmful genetic conditions. For either group, building a virtuous society requires a careful nurturing of character – caution for one and creativity for the other. Ethics is more about character-formation than ethical decision-making.

## POINTS IN COMMON

In practice, as already mentioned, these styles of ethical argument are often mixed together. Few of us avoid consequences altogether and, on global issues such as human-induced climate change, we would be very foolish to do so. It is also very difficult to avoid principles altogether. Talk of 'happiness' in terms of consequences, or 'love' in terms of personal situations, both look suspiciously like principles creeping in through a different route. And those who adopt a virtue-ethic style, in practice, often *do* engage in ethical decision-making. In public debates these styles of argument, while distinct, are often not treated as being mutually exclusive.

These styles of ethical argument are also to be found side-by-side within many accounts of Christian ethics. In Chapter 1 it will be seen that natural law approaches to Christian ethics make considerable use of principles and variously depict some forms of behaviour as 'natural' and (in more theological terms) 'God-given' and others as 'unnatural' or even 'sinful'. 'Happiness' or, more profoundly, 'well-being' is also very important for this approach to Christian ethics. And, of course, what could be more important within Christian ethics than a virtue such as 'love' or deep 'compassion'?

In reading the Gospels, all these approaches can be found at one point or another in the reported life and teaching of Jesus. Indeed, within the Sermon on the Mount all are present in Jesus's most distinctive and striking ethical command:

> You have heard that it was said, 'You shall love your neighbour [*a principle*] and hate your enemy.' But I say to you, Love your enemies and pray for those who persecute you [*a personal situation and a virtue*], so that you may be children of your Father in heaven [*a consequence*]; for he makes his sun rise on the evil and on the good, and sends rain on the righteous and on the unrighteous (Matthew 5.43–45).

The principle 'you shall love your neighbour' comes straight from the Tanakh (Jewish Bible) (Leviticus 19.18) and is expanded and not denied by the command to 'love your enemies'. 'Love your enemies,' in turn, is contextualised by Jesus telling his followers to 'pray for those who persecute you'. And the consequence that Jesus offers them is 'that you may be children of your Father in heaven', albeit without him promising them any special benefit here on earth.

## WHAT IS DISTINCTIVE ABOUT CHRISTIAN ETHICS?

If these four styles of ethical argument can be found in many different ethics traditions – secular and religious – what is it about Christian ethics that makes it distinctive?

In Chapter 1 it will be seen that Christian ethicists do not agree with each other about how their discipline is distinctive. Some see Christian ethics as being sharply different from other forms of ethics or, indeed, as *the only* valid form of ethics, whereas others accept that there are many continuities across faith traditions and that there are also frameworks shared with secular traditions. As result, some Christian ethicists readily co-operate with their secular colleagues on ethical issues, whereas others regard such co-operation as a betrayal. This is tricky territory within Christian ethics.

One way of understanding the differences here is to examine the distinctive appeals that Christian ethicists actually use in reaching ethical decision-making – that is, appeals which their non-Christian colleagues are less likely to make.

Framed in this way, at least four distinctive appeals are variously made by Christian ethicists: appeals to the Bible; appeals to Christian tradition; appeals to Christian experience; and appeals to Christian doctrine.

## APPEALS TO THE BIBLE

At its sharpest, if it is claimed that *the only* valid way to make an ethical decision is to base it *solely* upon biblical teaching (New Testament and Old Testament), then secular ethics and non-Christian religious ethics are both ruled out as irrelevant at the outset. The duty of the Christian is then to withdraw from the world or to convert the world. The Christian cannot validate anything meaningful within other ethical systems. On this understanding, to be ethical you must first be a Christian. Chapter 1 will look at Reformed Christian proponents of this position.

Catholic, Orthodox, Methodist, Presbyterian and Anglican Christian ethicists have seldom adopted this sharp position. Most of them do take appeals to the Bible seriously, and cite biblical texts frequently, but they also believe that the Bible is an important but not sufficient resource for ethical decision-making. Many of them are persuaded that biblical texts present a number of challenges.

Matthew 5.43–45 can be used again to illustrate some of these challenges. This passage from the New Testament quotes directly from the Tanakh (Jewish Bible). Christians tend to call the latter 'the Old Testament', whereas Jews – who often object to this term because it implies that their holy book is superseded by 'the New Testament' – prefer to call it the Hebrew Bible. Actually the term 'Hebrew Bible' has problems for Christian scholars because New Testament authors tend to quote from a much later Greek translation-come-interpretation of the original text of the Tanakh (which, to make matters even more complicated, contains some Aramaic as well as Hebrew).

None of this matters very much for this particular quotation, namely the principle 'you shall love your neighbour'. But it does matter in other contexts. What is more confusing is that the second half of this quotation, namely 'and hate your enemy', does not come directly from any version of the Tanakh (Hebrew or Greek). At most it is an allusion to some of the hostile remarks of, say, the Psalms to enemies. So, a biblical text is combined here with a biblical allusion or interpretation.

It can be seen from this that direct appeals to the Bible face two immediate and obvious problems: the problem of language (Greek or Hebrew) and the problem of interpretation. Yet from a perspective within Christian ethics there is also a much larger problem: does the expansion of a half-biblical quote given here by Jesus to 'love your enemies and pray for those who persecute you' imply that all Christians should be pacifists? That is indeed a difficult question and needs to be explored carefully in Chapter 3.

Added to the difficulties of language and interpretation is the problem of establishing a reliable biblical text. Because biblical manuscripts, long before printing, were copied out by hand for hundreds of years, variations were soon introduced (some probably deliberate but others not). The celebrated story of the woman taken in adultery in John 8, for example, has often been used within Christian ethics, sometimes in relation to Matthew 5.43–45. Unfortunately, the John 8 story seems to have been added to the Gospel later – in the earliest Greek manuscripts of John it is simply absent.

Another problem with Matthew 5.43–45 involves weighting. There are other texts in the Gospels that record strong anger, fierce denunciations and even an act of symbolic violence (overturning the table of the money-changers in the Temple) by Jesus. How are these to be weighed alongside Matthew 5.43–45? And if the invocations to annihilate enemies in Deuteronomy or Joshua are added to this, the overall weighting becomes even more difficult. Is there a danger of **cherry-picking** here? Is there a risk that Christian ethicists might be inclined to pick and choose texts that they like and ignore those they do not? Appeals to the Bible can all too soon become highly selective.

## APPEALS TO CHRISTIAN TRADITION

One way of overcoming some of these problems is to establish an authoritative tradition that regulates which parts of the Bible are to be given the greatest respect and that also regulates how they are to be interpreted. Within Judaism, Catholicism and Islam (which has gone to some lengths to suppress variant texts) there are such long-established traditions, albeit with dissenting traditions within each of them.

This may work up to a point, but it does so by deferring internal debate about sacred texts to these authorities. Within Presbyterianism, Methodism and Anglicanism, say, there are certainly well-respected leaders of the past, but none is typically regarded as binding upon their members.

An obvious point of conflict is that many (perhaps most) ancient sacred texts tend to contain contradictions.

For example, in the first three Gospels there is a crucial difference between them about giving away what you possess. In Mark, the earliest Gospel, as Jesus was setting out on a journey a man ran up, knelt before him and asked, 'Good Teacher, what must I do to inherit eternal life?' (Mark 10.17). After some discussion Jesus concluded: 'You lack one thing; go, sell what you own, and give [the money] to the poor, and you will have treasure in heaven; then come, follow me' (vs 21).

Both Matthew and Luke's Gospel knew Mark's Gospel, and Matthew at this point follows Mark quite closely. However, Luke significantly adds an extra word to Jesus's conclusion: 'sell *all* that you own and distribute [the money] to the poor' (Luke 18.22). There is a world of difference between giving away your possessions (as many of us do when we give away our redundant books, say, to Oxfam) and giving away *all* your possessions.

Or to take another example, in the same chapter of Mark, Jesus was asked about whether he considered divorce to be lawful. Again, after some discussion, he concluded unambiguously that, 'Whoever divorces his wife and marries another commits adultery against her; and if she divorces her husband and marries another, she commits adultery' (vs 11–12).

Matthew includes this story but changes the conclusion to, 'whoever divorces his wife, except for unchastity, and marries another commits adultery' (Matthew 19.9). The addition of 'except for unchastity' makes this conclusion much more ambiguous than that in Mark and has generated huge debates and a variety of different policies within world-wide Christianity.

It will be seen in Chapter 6 that the Eastern Orthodox Church, for instance, has a surprisingly liberal attitude towards divorce, allowing members to marry in church even after two divorces. The Catholic Church, in contrast, allows a marriage in church only after the annulment of a marriage, not a divorce. Some Baptist Churches have very strict policies against marriage after divorce, but others, while remaining more conservative on other ethical issues, do not. In Britain, Methodist leaders accepted marriage after divorce long before Anglicans.

The confusion here seems to have happened fairly early in the history of Christianity. Evidence for this can be seen within some of the early (but not the earliest) Greek manuscripts of the Gospels. These add the stern words 'and he who marries a divorced woman commits adultery' to Matthew's text.

In exploring appeals to tradition within Christian history there are some theologians who are difficult to ignore. In the chapters that follow, three are singled out as being especially influential: Augustine of Hippo, Thomas Aquinas and Martin Luther. These three voluminous theological geniuses represent three of the most crucial phases of Christianity: the adoption of Christianity as a Roman state religion; medieval Christendom; and the Protestant Reformation. Their continuing influence upon present-day Christian ethics will soon become apparent.

## APPEALS TO CHRISTIAN EXPERIENCE

Within those forms of Christianity that are suspicious of authoritative tradition, appeals to individual experience can be particularly attractive. They give a distinctively Christian take to the style of ethical argument that favours individual feelings, conscience or love. Such an appeal can be found among Quakers in the 17th century, among mystics throughout the history of Christianity, and especially among South American radical Pentecostals today.

A strong emphasis upon the 'inner light' of individual conscience was an important feature of the teaching of George Fox, the founder of the Quaker movement. He declared to the jury at Lancaster Assizes in 1664 that, 'I was a man of tender conscience, and if they had any sense of a tender conscience, they would consider that it was in obedience to Christ's commands that I could not swear'. Members of the Society of Friends, or Quakers, today tend to be reticent about making dogmatic ethical or doctrinal claims, leaving such matters to individual conscience and valuing collective silence punctuated by free-ranging individual testimonies in their Sunday meetings.

In contrast, radical Pentecostals favour exuberant enthusiasm rather than silence within services, but are equally suspicious of hierarchical religious authority. The radical growth of Pentecostalism in South America within the last two generations has transformed religious belonging in previously Catholic countries and has an emphasis upon gifts of the Spirit. In contrast to Catholic congregations subject to the authority of Rome, radical Pentecostals have relied heavily upon individual experience as their authority. As a result, radical Pentecostalism has managed to have considerable global growth, enthusiasm *and* numerous internal divisions.

Both Quakers and Pentecostals have some similarities with individual mystics who have been a feature of Christianity (and many other faith traditions) from the outset. There are clear signs of mysticism in some of Paul's letters in the New Testament, particularly in this celebrated autobiographical passage:

> I know a person in Christ who fourteen years ago was caught up to the third heaven—whether in the body or out of the body I do not know; God knows. And I know that such a person—whether in the body or out of the body I do not know; God knows— was caught up into Paradise and heard things that are not to be told, that no mortal is permitted to repeat. On behalf of such a one I will boast, but on my own behalf I will not boast, except of my weaknesses (2 Corinthians 12.2–5).

In an earlier letter Paul drew out the ethical implications of such an intense mystical experience in this seminal passage:

> When I was a child, I spoke like a child, I thought like a child, I reasoned like a child; when I became an adult, I put an end to childish

> ways. For now we see in a mirror, dimly, but then we will see face to face. Now I know only in part; then I will know fully, even as I have been fully known. And now faith, hope, and love abide, these three; and the greatest of these is love (1 Corinthians 13.11–13).

Of course, individual experience, conscience and love are features of most forms of Christianity and, as will be seen later, important constituents of many forms of Christian ethics. However, within these three forms of Christian belonging they are especially prominent. Arguably they provide the passion that can motivate Christian ethical behaviour, especially in its most radical and altruistic form, namely to 'love your enemies and pray for those who persecute you'.

While inspiring ethical passion and motivation, individual conscience can also generate divisions. Pentecostal groups world-wide have had to cope with many internal divisions at congregational level, sometimes on ethical issues on which members passionately disagree with each other. A new leader arises and divides an existing congregation. Exuberant passion inspires but can also divide.

In contrast, an emphasis upon experience can sometimes evoke a sense of unity between different faith traditions. In Asia, for example, there have been many discussions, for at least the last two centuries, between Catholic and Buddhist mystics about similarities in their forms of meditation and ethical practice. They claim to find similarities of experience despite their holding radically different beliefs about the existence of a personal God.

One final point about appeals to Christian experience: increasingly within Christian ethics it is realised that accounts of experience need to be contextualised. Experience is related to who you are and where you belong. Feminist Christian ethics raises questions about patriarchy within the discipline. Womanist Christian ethics raises additional questions about ethnicity and prejudice. Post-colonial Christian ethics raises questions about imperialism and power. Queer Christian ethics raises questions about discrimination and equality. Ecological Christian ethics raises questions about the environment and the treatment of animals. Disability Christian ethics raises questions about what is considered to be 'normal' and about the experience of being disadvantaged within society.

When these and other different experiences are identified within Christian ethics it becomes a much more interesting, relevant and challenging discipline. Once it might have been assumed that Christian ethicists were typically male, Western, abled and straight. Today a much wider spectrum of voiced experiences is to be heard within the discipline.

## APPEALS TO CHRISTIAN DOCTRINE

Within recent Christian ethics there has been a renewed emphasis upon theology. To return to this point, it is claimed that Christian ethics should be first and foremost a theological discipline, analysing the implications of how Christian doctrine shapes ethical decision-making.

This approach is often combined with a sharp critique of those forms of Christian ethics that are seen to 'collaborate' with secular forms of ethical discussion. The Christian ethicist should, so it is claimed, act as a prophetic witness to secular colleagues and strongly resist any secular assumptions about ethics. Conversion, not collaboration, should then be the central focus of the discipline.

There can be little doubt that this renewed emphasis has brought fresh energy to the discipline. Chapter 1 will explore some of it in more detail. At this point it is worth noting two broad issues.

The first is that an appeal to doctrine does respond to one of the difficulties faced by a purely biblical approach to Christian ethics, namely how to address ethical issues that are never mentioned in the Bible. To take an obvious area, many of the issues arising within bioethics today – such as human gene editing (just mentioned), storing human bio-data, and human stem cell therapy – are understandably not discussed in any biblical text. At most, the Christian ethicist can attempt to infer how biblical teaching on other issues *might* be relevant.

In contrast, a theological approach could start from the Christian doctrines of creation, redemption and sanctification. How can these specifically Christian doctrines respond to ethical issues arising within bioethics? Genes, bio-data and stem cells are all parts of human beings created in the image of God, redeemed in Christ and sanctified by the Holy Spirit. In contrast, some secular approaches to genes, bio-data and stem cells regard them simply as commodities to be manipulated, used or discarded at will.

Such a theological approach does not answer all of the detailed questions raised by bioethicists in these areas. However, it might at least generate some caution for Christians engaged with them.

The second broad issue arises directly from the first. Doctrinal appeals within Christian ethics – based upon, say, creation, redemption and sanctification – are unlikely to influence non-Christians, let alone those who see themselves as purely secular. If Christian ethicists are to have any public role – say on a national or regional medical ethics committee – they may feel they need to frame their contributions in less theological terms. Here is the dilemma. If they do not, they will probably not be heard; if they do, they may well be accused of reducing Christian ethics to secular ethics.

One way of partially resolving this dilemma is to engage in what is increasingly termed 'Abrahamic ethics'. Judaism, Christianity and Islam all recognise Abraham as a key patriarch or prophet – hence the name Abrahamic ethics. Proponents of this approach argue that there are broad doctrines held in common by all three of these faith traditions. For instance, all three hold that the world is created by an all-compassionate God. They obviously do not agree about the divine status of Jesus, but they might agree upon some of the values that Jesus shared with Judaism and that are also enshrined within the Qur'an.

In my own writings I have suggested four such values: compassion, care, faith/trust and humility. Although I derive these four values from the accounts in the Gospels of Jesus healing, I acknowledge that they can also be found more widely in other faith traditions, especially within Judaism and Islam. Some of them, at least, can also be found within those forms of secular humanism that were shaped initially by a Christian culture (albeit shorn of any reference to God). And compassion is particularly important within Buddhism.

Some Christian ethicists go further than this and argue that one version or another of the so-called Golden Rule ('do to others as you would have them do to you') can be found in all of the major faith traditions, including those of India, China and Japan, with or without a belief in God.

## COMBINING APPROACHES

It should be evident by now that these four appeals – to the Bible, to Christian tradition, to Christian experience and to Christian doctrine – need not be mutually exclusive. Almost every Christian ethicist will make some appeal to the Bible, but only some claim *solely* to appeal to the Bible. Different denominations variously weight Christian tradition, but most accounts of Christian ethics do pay at least some attention to tradition. Accounts of motivation within Christian ethics typically make at least some mention of Christian experience. Finally, Christian and, increasingly, Abrahamic doctrine features in many works in Christian ethics. Once more this is about emphasis not exclusivity.

## FURTHER READING

I expand the framework set out in this Introduction more fully in *A Textbook of Christian Ethics* (4th edition, London: T&T Clark, 2014).

My particular take on healthcare ethics can be found in my *Health Care and Christian Ethics* (Cambridge: Cambridge University Press, 2006) and discussion of the Golden Rule and Abrahamic ethics can be found in my *Moral Passion and Christian Ethics* (Cambridge: Cambridge University Press, 2017). However, both books, part of New Studies in Christian Ethics, are at advanced level. Of the 40 or so books in this series, the following are the most recent:

Barrera, Albino (2005), *Economic Compulsion and Christian Ethics*.
Barrera, Albino (2011), *Market Complicity and Christian Ethics*.
Bash, Anthony (2007), *Forgiveness and Christian Ethics*.
Cahill, Lisa Sowle (2013), *Global Justice, Christology and Christian Ethics*.
Cook, Christopher C.H. (2006), *Alcohol, Addiction and Christian Ethics*.
Deane-Drummond, Celia (2006), *Genetics and Christian Ethics*.
Elliot, David (2017), *Hope and Christian Ethics*.
McKenny, Gerald (2018), *Biotechnology and Christian Ethics*.
Mitchell, Jolyon (2007), *Media Violence and Christian Ethics*.
Pope, Stephen J. (2007), *Human Evolution and Christian Ethics*.
Scherz, Paul (2019), *Science and Christian Ethics*.
Sullivan-Dunbar, Sandra (2017), *Human Dependency and Christian Ethics*.
Tollefsen, Christopher O. (2014), *Lying and Christian Ethics*.

There are several well-received collections on Christian ethics, all with significant contributors (some more accessible than others), including:

Cahill, Lisa Sowle & Childress, James F. (eds) (1996), *Christian Ethics: Problems and Prospects* (Cleveland, OH: Pilgrim Press).

Hauerwas, Stanley & Wells, Samuel (eds) (2004), *The Blackwell Companion to Christian Ethics* (Oxford and New York: Blackwell).

Meilaender, Gilbert & Werpehowski, William (eds) (2007), *The Oxford Handbook of Theological Ethics* (Oxford & New York: Oxford University Press).

Gill, Robin (ed) (2012), *The Cambridge Companion to Christian Ethics* (2nd edition, Cambridge: Cambridge University Press).

Useful and up-to-date collections on religious ethics and Abrahamic religions are: William Schweiker (ed), *The Blackwell Companion to Religious Ethics* (Malden, MA and Oxford: Blackwell, 2005) and Adam J. Silverstein & Guy G. Stroumsa (eds), *The Oxford Handbook of the Abrahamic Religions* (Oxford: Oxford University Press, 2015).

The literature on religiously inspired violence grows all the time. However, the following collections are, again, very useful (but, again, some articles are more accessible than others): Mark Juergensmeyer, Margo Kitts & Michael Jerryson (eds), *The Oxford Handbook of Religion and Violence* (Oxford: Oxford University Press, 2006) – with nine of its chapters reproduced less expensively in their *Violence and the World's Religious Traditions* (Oxford: Oxford University Press, 2017); Andrew Murphy (ed), *The Blackwell Companion to Religion and Violence* (Malden, MA and Oxford: Blackwell, 2011); and James R. Lewis (ed), *The Cambridge Companion to Religion and Terrorism* (Cambridge: Cambridge University Press, 2017). I summarise this literature in an accessible form in my *Killing in the Name of God: Addressing Religious Inspired Violence* (London: Theos, 2018) available online free at:

https://www.theosthinktank.co.uk/research/2018/07/11/killing-in-the-name-of-god-addressing-religiously-inspired-violence

# DIFFERENT METHODS WITHIN CHRISTIAN ETHICS

One of the sharpest divisions within Christian ethics involves **natural law**. To understand this abiding division it is important to go back to the classic works of **Thomas Aquinas** and **Martin Luther** and to appreciate why and how they are so different from each other. Catholic forms of Christian ethics today are still highly influenced by Aquinas's notion of natural law. And many forms of Reformed Christian ethics still share Luther's suspicion of natural law and his radical emphasis upon the Bible.

Starting with Aquinas:

Aquinas was born into a life of some privilege in about 1225. His father was a count living at the castle of Roccasecca at Aquino, between Naples and Rome. After school and university Aquinas defied his father by becoming a Dominican monk (a Catholic order still celebrated for its learning and teaching). Among his many writings, two massive works are particularly significant: first the *Summa Contra Gentiles* ('a treatise against heathens') and then, towards the end of his life, the *Summa Theologica* ('a theological treatise'). His highly influential understanding of natural law can be found in both of these works, although the first is more apologetic in intent than the second.

At the time, these two works were considered dangerous innovations, particularly because they made great use of the Greek philosopher Aristotle rather than the more widely accepted Plato. In both of his works Aquinas was concerned to show that the Christian faith rests upon a rational foundation. Aristotle's work, preserved in the Islamic world, provided him with the intellectual framework for this and avoided some of the theological speculations of Plato. Aquinas believed that Aristotle's naturalistic framework could indeed work harmoniously with Christian revelation.

Shortly before his death in 1274 he had a number of mystical experiences, including one while saying Mass – after which he stopped work on his *Summa Theologica*, saying that 'all I have written seems to me like so much straw compared with what I have seen and with what has been revealed to me'. He died in France on his way to a papal conference in Rome.

## NATURAL LAW IN THE *SUMMA THEOLOGICA*

*Summa Theologica* asks a series of questions about natural law, including:

- Whether all acts of virtue are prescribed by natural law?
- Whether natural law is the same for everyone?
- Whether natural law can be changed?
- Whether natural law can be abolished from the human heart?

### WHETHER ALL ACTS OF VIRTUE ARE PRESCRIBED BY NATURAL LAW?

Aquinas follows Aristotle in making a connection between natural law and virtue. Everything is inclined by natural law to a mode of operation that is suitable to its own form. For example, fire is inclined to give heat. Human beings, uniquely possessing a rational soul, are inclined by natural law to act according to (some) virtues and thus to promote their own well-being.

### WHETHER NATURAL LAW IS THE SAME FOR EVERYONE?

Aquinas follows Aristotle again in accepting that all human beings have some awareness of natural law and thus possess a natural tendency or inclination towards virtue and well-being. Primary principles about what is right or wrong can be known through the use of reason alone. Of course, human rationality can be distorted – human beings are fallible – but the theoretical principles of natural law are the same for everyone everywhere.

For example, Aquinas notes, theft is always wrong and against natural law, even though some in the ancient world did not recognise that it is so. He insists that we are all capable through reason of discovering that theft is wrong as a general principle. However, in particular cases restoring goods held in trust might be unreasonable if they were intended for use to fight against one's own country. In this context a failure to restore goods would not be theft.

So it is natural for human beings to act according to reason and, from their use of reason, to discern what is good and what is bad. Truth about primary or general principles is the same for everyone, whether everyone recognises this or not. Secondary principles, derived from the general principles and concerned with detailed action in changeable contexts, are also the same for most people. However, error, sin or bad customs may distort these secondary principles.

### WHETHER NATURAL LAW CAN BE CHANGED?

Aquinas makes a distinction here between change by addition and change by subtraction. He sees little problem with change by addition, noting that human and divine laws (which cannot be discerned solely through reason) may be added to natural law (which can be so discerned). Although humans cannot contradict natural law, they can sometimes add to it. God can indeed add to it.

Subtraction, however, is quite a different matter. Here, general or primary principles are unalterable and cannot be subtracted. Yet secondary principles may occasionally be changed by subtraction. To take the example of theft again; Aquinas argues that, since all things finally belong to God, taking something from another person on God's command would not be theft. More contentiously, he also argues that adultery – understood as sexual intercourse with another person's spouse – is always against reason and wrong, but, if such an act were to be commanded by God, it would not be wrong and it would not be adultery

### WHETHER NATURAL LAW CAN BE ABOLISHED FROM THE HUMAN HEART?

Aquinas insists that general or primary principles cannot be blotted out or abolished from the human heart. They are known, at least in the abstract, to all people. Human nature endures despite human sinfulness.

However, in practice, secondary principles, relying upon primary principles, can be blotted out or abolished by evil opinions, speculative errors, bad customs or corrupt habits.

## NATURAL LAW BEYOND THE *SUMMA THEOLOGICA*

In the chapters that follow, one more section of the *Summa Theologica* on natural law will be summarised (in Chapter 3 on war and peace). However, in Chapter 4 (on the environment) and in Chapter 6 (on sexuality) the sections will be summarised from the *Summa Contra Gentiles*. The latter demonstrate with particular clarity how Aquinas deployed natural law in the context of ethical decision-making. Together with one further source for Chapter 2 (on Princely Government) they demonstrate the strengths and some of the weaknesses of a style of ethics that has shaped papal teaching for centuries.

It will soon emerge that Aquinas's account of natural law faces a number of problems in the modern world in addition to its strengths.

### STRENGTHS

Defenders of natural law value it for its emphatic defence of ethical objectivity. According to Aquinas, general or primary principles are unchangeable and normative. Some things, such as theft, adultery and murder, are always wrong. That is, they are objectively wrong. They may clash with other principles at times, but they still remain wrong. Even today most people might agree that, say, genocide, child abuse and slavery are always wrong. That these abuses still happen in the modern world does not make them right. They have sometimes been justified in the past, but that still does not make them right. They are simply wrong.

Another point often made in favour of Aquinas is that he offers a clear path for coping with apparent exceptions. For him exceptions are not really exceptions at all. They are acts that are not what they appear to be. So theft, adultery and murder are always wrong, but if God were to command them in particular instances they would no longer be theft, adultery or murder. Recategorising an act when trying to cope with difficult cases is something that many of us still do. Juries, for example, frequently have to decide whether a particular killing is murder, manslaughter or simply an unfortunate accident.

A third point made about Aquinas is that he allows plenty of room for what today would be termed secular ethics. He emphatically does not claim that only Christians can be ethical. Natural law allows that all people everywhere can be ethical, whether they are Christians or not. Specifically, Christian ethics *adds* to, but does not *subtract* from, secular ethics (provided, of course, that secular ethics has been properly stated).

This position could be very attractive for those working in business ethics, bioethics or academic research ethics today. If the ethical principles identified in any of those areas applied only to Christians, non-Christians would simply be off the hook. Non-Christians working in business, medicine or academic research would not need to stick to any ethical requirements.

Yet it is doubtful if many people would be very impressed if their doctor informed them that, as she is not a Christian, there is no need for her to abide by ethical standards in medicine. They might well decide to change their doctor.

Finally, Aquinas offers a clear line of demarcation between philosophy and theology. As a theologian he uses the pre-Christian philosopher Aristotle to provide the philosophical framework for his natural law theory. However, he looks to Christian revelation to establish divine law beyond natural law. For him divine law never contradicts natural law: it adds, not subtracts. Grace crowns nature: grace does not destroy nature.

WEAKNESSES

Few philosophers today who are not themselves religious make much use of natural law theory. This is despite a renewed interest in ethical objectivity among recent philosophers. Natural law theory seems to have more appeal to Catholic ethicists than to most other ethicists. If someone already believes that God created the world and that God's good intentions are still evident within this creation, then natural law theory may have considerable appeal (despite the fact that Aristotle himself showed little interest in these beliefs).

A number of problems have been identified in Aquinas's account of natural law. The most obvious problem is getting agreement about the meaning and ethical significance of the word 'natural'. It will be seen in Chapters 4 and 6 that what he considers to be natural in terms of gender and sexuality is strongly contested today. For instance, he assumes that men by nature are more rational than women, that women are more rational than slaves, and that slaves are more rational than animals. Not exactly 21st century assumptions.

In addition, perhaps there are things today that many of us consider to be natural which will cause equal offence in 900 years' time – for example, our treatment of animals, our laxity about the environment, our resort to wars, or whatever. What is considered to be 'natural' does seem to have changed over time. Similarly, some medieval 'virtues', such as chivalry, no longer seem 'natural' today.

Another problem is that Aquinas (and Aristotle before him) sees 'well-being' as the final goal of human beings. Today it is very difficult to get agreement about what constitutes well-being. As already suggested, we might be able to get some narrow agreement about what is objectively wrong, but agreement on what is good for us appears to be much more elusive.

Then there is a problem that troubles both secular philosophers and some Reformed Christian ethicists – namely whether it really is appropriate to assume that what is 'natural' is also 'good'. Philosophers might argue (following Kant) that it is a mistake to derive an 'ought' from an 'is'. For them ethical claims cannot safely be derived from scientific descriptions.

To give a blunt example: among lions and some other mammals it is natural for a male to kill the young offspring of an unattached female before forcibly mating with her. When human males today emulate this particular piece of behaviour they are rewarded, if caught and convicted, not with a new pride but with a life sentence for murder and rape.

Some Reformed Christian ethicists also have a problem with assuming that what is 'natural' is also 'good', but for a very different reason. Their objection is theological. In a fallen world, so they argue, we can no longer discern God's intentions by observing God's creation. This creation is now too distorted by original and ongoing sin for humans to make any such discernment safely. Instead, people can only know about the good from God's revelation within the Bible.

This last point suggests a very different approach to ethics than the natural law approach of Aquinas. As already seen, Aquinas does recognise that sin distorts habits and customs and blinds people to what is good. Nevertheless, he still believes that human beings, however sinful, do retain a rational capacity to discern the good. Martin Luther (as will be seen in a moment) was not so convinced.

## NATURAL LAW IN MODERN CATHOLIC THOUGHT

A number of specific examples can be given of the various ways that Catholic theologians have responded positively to these criticisms of Aquinas.

Writing in his 1976 book *Aquinas*, the Jesuit philosopher and historian **F.C. Copleston** compares Aquinas to those secular philosophers, following David Hume, who argue that ethics is primarily about relative feelings and emotions rather than about objective rationality. Copleston concedes that Aquinas can sometimes appear too didactic and rational and that ethical principles do *appear to be* relative rather than absolute in the modern world.

However, he insists that Aquinas *was* aware of differing ethical perspectives across different human cultures (not least because 13th century Europe saw a flourishing of Islamic and Jewish thought from which Aquinas himself benefited). Yet that awareness in itself is no proof that ethical principles are actually relative. Some things may be objectively wrong, whether all human cultures recognise this or not. Indeed, Aquinas accepts that human cultures can be distorted by a variety of factors.

On the issue of ethics as emotion, Copleston does concede that emotion plays a part and points to the obvious example of euthanasia. Both a defender and a critic of euthanasia for a terminal patient in serious pain are likely to express passionate emotions. Nonetheless, he argues, establishing rational principles is still important in such an ethical debate. The crucial feature of Aquinas (who, after all, devoted considerable space in *Summa Theologica* to the passions) is that, unlike modern relativists, he did believe in ethical objectivity.

The publication by the philosopher **Alasdair MacIntyre** of *After Virtue* in 1981 has had a profound effect upon many Christian ethicists. MacIntyre goes beyond Copleston, arguing for a revolution in ethics by returning to Aristotle's **virtue ethics**. He contends that secular ethics is too committed to the idea that rational discussion can resolve ethical debates. In reality a debate on, say, abortion is incapable of rational resolution, with pro-choice and pro-life opponents locked into a debate involving opposite and irreducible principles. Much more important for MacIntyre are the virtues that shape both people's lives within particular communities *and* their supposedly rational principles.

An emphasis upon both ethical objectivity and virtue ethics can be seen in **Pope John-Paul II**'s 1993 encyclical *Veritatis Splendor*. This influential document argues that there is a 'crisis of moral truth' in the modern world, not least because of a radical clash of secular perspectives. One perspective, within ethics, has a strong emphasis upon personal freedom and autonomy, seeing individual conscience as the ultimate arbiter of what is right and wrong. The other perspective, within social science, regards individuals as being thoroughly conditioned by society and not free at all to make autonomous judgments.

The pope concludes:

> In such a context it is absolutely necessary to clarify, in the light of the word of God and the living Tradition of the Church, the fundamental notions of human freedom and of the moral law, as well as their profound and intimate relationship. Only thus will it be possible to respond to the rightful claims of human reason in a way which accepts the valid elements present in certain currents of contemporary moral theology without compromising the Church's heritage of moral teaching with ideas derived from an erroneous concept of autonomy (Pope John-Paul II, 1993: section 7).

In developing a less rigid version of natural law within Catholic Christian ethics it is well worth noting the writings of two American Catholic theologians, **Jean Porter** and **Lisa Sowle Cahill**. Porter is more philosophical in orientation and a recognised expert on Aquinas; Cahill is more highly involved in bioethics (as will be seen in Chapter 5), sexual ethics, Just War ethics and now ecological ethics. Both Christian ethicists have contributed significantly to the Cambridge University Press series *New Studies in Christian Ethics* (already mentioned in the Introduction).

In her 1995 book *Moral Action and Christian Ethics*, Jean Porter reacts against the straitjacket of Immanuel Kant's principled approach to ethics. Instead she argues for a subtle system of Christian ethics, expanding Aquinas, that has a tension between the following virtues: self-regard grounded in restraint and forthrightness; kindliness and decency built out of caring; and fairness and responsibility forming a basis for justice.

In her 2013 book *Global Justice, Christology and Christian Ethics*, Lisa Sowle Cahill argues that:

> Certain goods for humans can be universally known, most obviously those based on the physical conditions of human survival and our natural sociality and need for cooperative relationships. Moreover, basic human equality yields an obligation to ensure that all have access to the minimum conditions of human sustenance. This implies, at the very least, that our common human environment be protected as a prerequisite of human flourishing. The process of naming ecological goods and responding to ecological dangers should be inclusive of all those affected. A natural law approach to the characteristics and goods of 'nature' can be extended analogously from human to nonhuman beings. We can know some universal ecological goods, such as interdependence, balance of ecosystems, openness to the new, clean water and air, and species survival. As public goods or global common goods, these are at one level *human* goods. But they are also goods for *nature itself* (Cahill, 2013:281).

She recognises more frankly than many other Catholic ethicists that 'knowledge of the natural law is always perspectival and partial' and 'is never detached from the particular contexts, identities, and interests of knowing subjects' (2013:265).

Clearly natural law theory within Catholic Christian ethics is still developing. This will become particularly evident in Chapter 6 when discussing tensions within churches today about sexuality.

## MARTIN LUTHER

It is time now to turn to Martin Luther and to his followers. They offer a radically different approach to Christian ethics that is often highly suspicious of natural law and at odds with Aquinas – albeit increasingly with a renewed interest in virtue ethics.

Luther was born in Saxony in 1483 and, like Aquinas, joined a monastery as a young man and, like Aquinas, against his father's wishes. In 1507 he had a profound religious experience. He continued to teach biblical studies, but eventually came to the conclusion that through his own efforts alone he could not attain salvation.

Crucially, in 1517 he published his 95 theses in Wittenberg against the abuses created by the Church's sale of indulgences. The latter had been authorised by Pope Leo X, partly in order to finance the building of St Peter's in Rome. Luther refused to retract his theses despite strong papal pressure and was finally excommunicated by Pope Leo in 1520. It was in this year that he published his seminal *Treatise on Good Works*.

For the next 26 years, until his death in 1546, he worked hard translating the Bible, writing biblical commentaries, revising the liturgy, composing hymns, preaching and writing letters that were key to the extraordinary political and religious success of the Protestant Reformation throughout northern Europe.

### TREATISE ON GOOD WORKS

This small but highly influential document began life as a sermon for his congregation. *Treatise on Good Works* soon grew into a small book. Luther takes the final sentence of this biblical quotation concerned with the proprieties of eating and drinking as key:

> The faith that you have, have as your own conviction before God. Blessed are those who have no reason to condemn themselves because of what they approve. But those who have doubts are condemned if they eat, because they do not act from faith; for whatever does not proceed from faith is sin (Romans 14.22–23).

Luther argues that people can know when they do what is good or what is not good. If they find in their hearts confidence that it pleases God, the work is good. However, such firm confidence is possible only for a Christian who is enlightened and strengthened by grace. A 'heathen, a Jew, a Turk', in contrast, lacking faith knows no such confidence and can do only sinful works.

Those who have followed 'blind reason' and 'heathen ways' have set faith not above, but beside, other virtues. In contrast, it is faith alone that makes all other works good, acceptable and worthy. Without faith, works are sin.

As a result, all works become equal, and one is like another. All distinctions between works fall away, 'whether they be great, small, short, long, few or many'. Works are acceptable not for their own sake, but only because of the faith that generates them.

Luther offers a human example of this:

> When a man and a woman love and are pleased with each other, and thoroughly believe in their love, who teaches them how they are to behave, what they are to do, leave undone, say, not say, think? Confidence alone teaches them all this, and more. They make no difference in works: they do the great, the long, the much, as gladly as the small, the short, the little, and vice versa; and that too with joyful, peaceful, confident hearts, and each is a free companion of the other.

The Christian does whatever is required to be done, not to gather merit but cheerfully, freely and simply to please God. So no amount of fasting, confession, intercessions, monasteries or churches is worth anything without faith in God. Outward works without faith – such as papal bulls, seals, flags and indulgences – lead only to idolatry and hypocrisy. Luther firmly rejects all works that are done without faith.

Of course, faith does not forbid good works. Rather he states his position pithily as follows:

> In this way I have, as I said, always praised faith, and rejected all works which are done without such faith, in order thereby to lead men from the false, pretentious, pharisaic, unbelieving good works, with which all monastic houses, churches, homes, low and higher classes are over-filled, and lead them to the true, genuine, thoroughly good, believing works. In this no one opposes me except the unclean beasts, which do not divide the hoof, as the Law of Moses decrees; who will suffer no distinction among good works, but go lumbering along.

Luther then looks at the Ten Commandments and argues that each of these demonstrates the primacy of faith.

Just to take the First Commandment, he suggests the question: 'Why then do we have so many laws of the Church and of the State, and many ceremonies of churches, monastic houses, holy places, which urge and tempt men to good works, if faith does all things through the First Commandment?' He answers: 'Simply because we do not all have faith or do not heed it. If every man had faith, we would need no more laws, but every one would of himself at all times do good works, as his confidence in God teaches him.'

With his characteristic, but somewhat barbed, humour, he also suggests the question: 'How can I trust surely that all my works are pleasing to God, when at times I fall, and talk, eat, drink and sleep too much, or otherwise transgress, as I cannot help doing?' He answers: 'This question shows that you still regard faith as a work among other works, and do not set it above all works. For it is the highest work for this very reason, because it remains and blots out these daily sins by not doubting that God is so kind to you as to wink at such daily transgression and weakness.'

### STRENGTHS

Many Christians today, including Catholics, might acknowledge that some of the medieval religious practices were corrupt and that Luther's sharp criticisms of them were an important corrective. Just as Jesus, following many biblical prophets, sharply criticised the religious authorities of his day, so Luther did in his day.

A prophetic tradition condemning religious hypocrisy remains one of the abiding features of Christian ethics. Liberation theologians in parts of South America, followed by theologians in South Africa challenging apartheid, as well as the Confessing Church earlier in Nazi Germany, have all been important parts of this prophetic tradition.

In Western society today there is widespread concern about the self-protecting suppression of evidence about child abuse within churches. This remains an important task for Christian ethicists to challenge – despite churches' internal confusions about sexuality in the modern world.

Again, many Christians might applaud Luther's emphasis (following Paul) upon faith. Within ecumenical theology a doctrine of justification by faith, in one form or another, is widely held by Reformed and Catholic theologians alike. Seeing good works as a product of faith and as a response to God's love (and not as a means to gaining personal merit) would also be widely endorsed.

In addition, deploying the Bible to shape Christian ethics – just as Luther did so emphatically in *Treatise on Good Works* – would be regarded by most Christian ethicists today as essential. As mentioned in the Introduction, appeals to the Bible are made within Christian ethics across denominations. Indeed, it will be seen later that recent papal encyclicals make considerable use of the Bible.

## WEAKNESSES

The phrase 'a heathen, a Jew, a Turk' within this brief summary of *Treatise on Good Works* was quoted deliberately. In Chapter 7 it will be seen that there are deeply troubling signs of anti-Semitism within Luther's writings. These will be discussed later, but for the moment they act as a warning. Luther's casual, and sometimes explicit, anti-Semitism is more widely acknowledged within Christian ethics today than it was in the past.

However, the problem here is not simply anti-Semitism, egregious though that is. There is also the crucial problem of how Christian ethics relates to other forms of religious or secular ethics. Luther seems to be drawing a very sharp line between good works done by Christians acting through faith and the 'good' works of everyone else. As a result, non-Christian good works are regarded as not good at all. They are simply regarded as sinful.

In contrast, Aquinas evidently endorses good works (religious or secular) as products of natural law. Luther, however, seems to preclude this option altogether. Although he occasionally mentions natural law, Luther typically does not regard it as authoritative. This is a strong tension that continues to divide Christian ethicists today.

Another tension involves Luther's appeal to the Bible. One highly significant feature of the Protestant Reformation is known by the Latin tag *sola Scriptura* (solely Scripture). The force of this is to claim that it is *only* the Bible that should be used to determine what is right and what is wrong. Nothing else should be regarded as authoritative for the Christian. The authority of the Bible is absolute.

There is much dispute about whether or not Luther himself was making such a claim as strongly as this. *Treatise on Good Works* does indeed use the Bible to show that faith rather than good works is key to the Christian life. However, it will be seen later that, in reality, Luther makes appeals to Christian (and sometimes secular) tradition and experience when arguing about a particular issue. And, even in *Treatise on Good Works*, it will be evident from the summary above that he does use an analogy from human marriage.

Two years after writing *Treatise on Good Works* Luther famously depicted the Epistle of James as 'an epistle of straw' when compared to Romans, Galatians, Ephesians, 1 Peter and 1 John. For him, at that time at least (he withdrew these words later), James 'has nothing of the nature of the gospel about it'. It does seem, then, that Luther did not regard all parts of the Bible as being equally authoritative. Some sort of (perhaps non-biblical) selectivity – or **cherry-picking** – seems to have been implicit here.

It is not difficult to see why Luther was so disdainful of James. Consider this passage:

> What good is it, my brothers and sisters, if you say you have faith but do not have works? Can faith save you? If a brother or sister is naked and lacks daily food, and one of you says to them, 'Go in peace; keep warm and eat your fill', and yet you do not supply their bodily needs, what is the good of that? So faith by itself, if it has no works, is dead. But someone will say, 'You have faith and I have works.' Show me your faith without works, and I by my works will show you my faith. You believe that God is one; you do well. Even the demons believe— and shudder. Do you want to be shown, you senseless person, that faith without works is barren? Was not our ancestor Abraham justified by works when he offered his son Isaac on the altar? (James 2.14–21).

At face value this passage seems to be quite opposite to *Treatise on Good Works*. The rhetorical question 'Can faith save you?' presumably expects the answer 'no' in James, whereas Luther would surely give it an emphatic 'yes'. Again, it is not clear that Luther would wholly endorse the claim that 'faith by itself, if it has no works, is dead'. And it is doubtful if he would have deemed

'Abraham justified [solely] by works' – an assumption that, arguably, is implicit within James.

## REFORMED CHRISTIAN ETHICS FOLLOWING LUTHER

Here are two examples that illustrate the contrasting ways that Reformed theologians have responded positively to these criticisms of Luther.

The writings of the Lutheran theologian **Dietrich Bonhoeffer** are especially poignant. Executed in 1945 at the age of 39 by the Nazis, his heroic return to Germany in 1935 has long been admired by Christian ethicists. At the time he declared: 'I shall have no right to participate in the reconstruction of Christian life in Germany after the war if I do not share the trials of this time with my people.'

His book *Ethics* was written at the very outset of the Second World War. It reflects his love of Karl Barth's theology and his own passionate Christian commitment. At the outset he states bluntly:

> The knowledge of good and evil seems to be the aim of all ethical reflection. The first task of Christian ethics is to invalidate this knowledge. In launching this attack on the underlying assumptions of all other ethics, Christian ethics stands so completely alone that it becomes questionable whether there is any purpose in speaking of Christian ethics at all (Bonhoeffer, 1955:3).

He meditates upon the Fall of humanity in Genesis and sees in this a radical disunion between human beings and God: 'Theirs eyes were opened' (Genesis 3.7). Having known only good before the Fall, he insists, they now know good and evil. Even human conscience and a quest for self-knowledge are then deeply distorted by sin. Only in Christ can we overcome this. Hence the sharp divide between secular ethics and Christian ethics. In his account of Christian ethics it is the Bible that is his central authority.

Bonhoeffer articulates a form of **command ethics** combined with a style of ethical argument based upon personal situations. This was suspicious of the principled approach of Aquinas and saw Christian ethics as focused upon God's commands within the Bible. So in his youthful 1929 book, later translated as *No Rusty Swords*, he argues that: 'there are not and cannot be Christian norms and principles of a moral nature; the concepts of "good" and "evil" exist only in the performance of an action, i.e. at any specific present, and hence any attempt to lay down principles is like trying to draw a bird in flight' (Bonhoeffer, 1965:36). As a result:

there are no actions which are bad in themselves – even murder can be justified – there is only faithfulness to God's will or deviation from it ... we can give no generally valid decisions which we might then hold out to be the only Christian one, because in so doing we are only setting out new principles and coming into conflict with the law of freedom. Rather can we only seek to be brought into the concrete situation of the decision and to show one of the possibilities of decision which present themselves at that point (Bonhoeffer, 1965:41–42).

For Bonhoeffer it is 'the will of God' that is paramount in Christian ethics: 'there is no other law than the law of freedom ... the new commandments of Jesus can never be regarded merely as ethical principles' (1965:40–41).

In recent Christian ethics it is the Christian philosopher **John Hare** who has done much to defend and extend **command ethics**. In his 2015 book *God's Command*, Hare offers an extensive defence of the claim that what makes something obligatory is that God commands it, and what makes something wrong is that God forbids it.

For example, using this command approach to Christian ethics, the requirement by Jesus to 'Love your enemies and pray for those who persecute you' (Matthew 5.44) gives Christians a very particular and demanding sense of obligation. It is good to love your enemies and it is good to pray for those who persecute you.

Hare has been critical of secular ethicists who miss this point, arguing that a belief in God addresses an important gap in many secular accounts of ethical obligation. Why should we finally feel obliged to help others beyond our own narrow self-interest? What accounts for a strong sense of altruism and what motivates genuine altruism?

Interestingly for an Evangelical Christian, in *God's Command* Hare extends his account of command ethics into Judaism and Islam alongside Christianity. In all three **Abrahamic faiths** he claims divine command is crucial:

God's command ... produces not only *moral* obligations, but obligations of other kinds: in Judaism, for example, ceremonial and dietary
obligations; in Christianity, obligations about baptism and Eucharist; in
Islam, obligations about pilgrimage and daily prayer (Hare, 2015:25).

## TWO RADICAL FORMS OF CHRISTIAN ETHICS

Other Christian ethicists have extended Bonhoeffer's objection to
principles in ethics and his emphasis upon personal situations.
**Joseph Fletcher** and **Don Cupitt** are two of the most prominent
and radical Christian ethicists to do so.

Joseph Fletcher's 1966 book *Situation Ethics* received considerable attention when it was published. In summary, it argues
that love should direct our moral behaviour to each other and
love properly understood cannot readily be captured by ethical
principles. For Jews, Christians and Muslims alike, love (or
compassion) derives from a conviction that God first loves (or
shows compassion to) us, so we in turn should show love
(or show compassion) to each other *and* (some today would
add) to the rest of God's creation:

> *Christian* situation ethics has only one norm or principle or law (call it
> what you will) that is binding and unexceptionable, always good and
> right regardless of the circumstances. That is 'love' – the *agape* of the
> summary commandment to love God and the neighbour. Everything
> else without exception, all laws and rules and principles and ideals
> and norms, are only *contingent*, only valid *if they happen* to serve love
> in any situation (Fletcher, 1966:30–31).

He puts the first word here in italics because he wants to emphasise
that a non-Christian may have a norm that is different from 'love' or
*agape*. Such a person would, in his view, still be a situationist but not
a Christian situationist. (In retirement he became a secular humanist
himself, so he might have changed his mind on this point.)

Fletcher explains that this position involves some form of ethical
relativism:

> It is necessary to insist that situation ethics is willing to make full and
> respectful use of principles, to be treated as maxims but not as laws

or precepts. We might call it 'principled relativism'. To repeat the term used above, principles or maxims or general rules are *illuminators*. But they are not *directors*. The classic rule of moral theology has been to follow laws but to do it *as much as possible* according to love and according to reason ... Situation ethics, on the other hand, calls upon us to keep law in a subservient place, so that *only* love and reason really count when the chips are down! (Fletcher, 1966:31).

Fletcher returns to the issue of relativism at several points in *Situation Ethics*, aware perhaps that this was its most vulnerable feature. At one point he claims that 'the situationist avoids words like "never" and "perfect" and "always" and "complete" as he avoids the plague' (1966:43–44). Or again: 'No twentieth-century man of even average training will turn his back on the anthropological and psychological evidence for relativity in morals. There are no "universal laws" held by all men everywhere at all times, no consensus of all men' (1966:76).

He is, at least partially, aware that 'to be relative, of course, means to be relative *to* something ... to be "absolutely relative" (an uneasy combination of terms) is to be inchoate, random, unpredictable, unjudgeable, meaningless, amoral' (1966.44). But he still faces an obvious problem: if someone claims, for example, that 'everything is relative', then that person might expect someone else to ask whether that claim itself is relative and, if it is, how it can then be trusted. This is a running problem in *Situation Ethics* because it makes so many dogmatic claims about situationism.

His own 'solution' to this dilemma is to make another dogmatic claim: 'There must be an absolute or norm of some kind if there is to be any true relativity' (1966:44). But note the word 'true' in this claim. Later he avoids this word and uses, instead, the term 'the highest good':

Nothing is intrinsically good but the highest good. The *summum bonum* [highest good], the end or purpose of all ends – love. We cannot say anything we do *is* good, only that it is a means to an end and therefore *happens* in that cause-and-effect relation to have value (Fletcher, 1966:129).

Don Cupitt's 1995 book *Solar Ethics* takes this ethical relativism further. In his earlier writings, such as his 1971 book *Christ and the Hiddenness of God*, he takes a position within Christian ethics that is similar to Fletcher's. However, in *Solar Ethics* he adopts the **non-realist approach** to ethics that has characterised his writings since the publication in 1980 of his book *Taking Leave of God*.

Cupitt takes issue in *Solar Ethics* with ethicists (religious or secular) for 'clinging to moral realism or objectivism long after that belief has become manifestly untenable'. Instead he believes that ethics should, like the Sun, simply be 'its own outpouring self-expression'. For Cupitt there is 'no objective moral order' and 'the entire vocabulary of the rational soul, conscience, the will, the moral law and so on is *dead*'.

At times he still depicts himself as a 'Christian' non-realist, while dissociating himself from any metaphysical convictions:

> There is nothing left for ethics to be but that we should love life and pour out our hearts – and that is emotivism or solar ethics. As the man says, 'You are the light of the world' (Matt. 5.14). For solar ethics is a version of Christian ethics, if one may say so (Cupitt, 1995:6–9).

## EMERGING CONTEXTUAL METHODS WITHIN CHRISTIAN ETHICS

In the Introduction it was mentioned that a number of other contextualised versions within Christian ethics are currently emerging and developing. Among them are:

- Feminist Christian ethics raising questions about patriarchy within the discipline.
- Womanist Christian ethics raising additional questions about ethnicity and prejudice.
- Post-colonial Christian ethics raising questions about imperialism and power.
- Queer Christian ethics raising questions about discrimination and equality.
- Ecological Christian ethics raising questions about the environment and the treatment of animals.

- Disability Christian ethics raising questions about what is considered to be 'normal' and about the experience of being disadvantaged within society.

The most developed of these is **feminist Christian ethics**. A particularly important book, written in 1996, on this approach is **Susan Frank Parsons'** *Feminism and Christian Ethics*. The value of this book, also written for the series *New Studies in Christian Ethic*, is that it identifies three different paradigms within feminist Christian ethics (and within secular ethics).

The first is the liberal paradigm with roots in the enlightenment. On its basis many of the early feminists argued for equality of rights and respect. As with other forms of liberalism it focuses upon rational individualism and personal autonomy and struggles with social justice and communitarianism.

The second is the social constructionist paradigm and has roots in Marxism. The focus here is upon eliminating patriarchal social structures and creating a new social order. In turn it struggles with an emphasis upon personal autonomy.

The third is the naturalist paradigm with a focus upon innate biological differences between men and women, especially differences resulting from child-bearing. Aspects of philosophy, social science and biology are used to depict these three paradigms.

Parsons notes that, although these three paradigms are distinct, in practice they are often combined:

> Perhaps one of the clearest illustrations of this comes from those feminists who identify with the social constructionist task of investigating the impact of structures upon the shaping of human consciousness, but who at the same time believe with liberals that there is an authentic nature within us, shared in common with men, which can only be fulfilled through a just social order.
>
> In other cases, the work of feminists is contradictory ... the obvious example is of those feminists who work within the naturalist paradigm, believing there to be a distinctive nature of women which feminist ethical thinking can enunciate, which exactly runs counter to the postmodern feminist claim that there is no such thing as a given nature (Parsons, 1996:175).

A variation on this approach is **womanist Christian ethics**. Inspired by the writings of Alice Walker in the 1980s, black theologians, especially in the United States, have explored black narratives and lives, with a particular focus upon those coming out of the experience of slavery. In a context of radical discrimination based upon colour, the first and second of Parsons' paradigms are highly relevant to this approach to Christian ethics.

A good example of womanist Christian ethics is **Kelly Brown Douglas**'s 1994 book *The Black Christ*, reprinted in 2019 in a 25th anniversary edition. Douglas traces the roots of this approach to slave Christianity and then to the black-nationalist activism especially of Martin Luther King and Malcolm X in the United States. She sees significant ethical tensions within the approach between liberation and reconciliation and between violent and non-violent action.

Douglas argues that a womanist approach to Christian ethics is still highly relevant today. Recent mass murders by white supremacists in black churches and synagogues demonstrate this clearly for her. She sees this approach as an ongoing challenge both to white churches and to society at large.

**Post-colonial Christian ethics** broadens the womanist approach to include all those who have been affected by colonialism – men as well as women. The work of the Indian Catholic theologian **Susan Abraham** is a useful guide to this approach.

Since she now teaches in the United States, she is conscious that her own theological interests in Hindu-Christian dialogue and those of her Indian Hindu colleagues are often regarded as 'contextualised' and peripheral by her other theological colleagues. In contrast, 'white, Euro-American Protestant or Christian or Atheist colleagues [imagine that they] are able to do "objective" and academic Hinduism'.

Abraham uses recent perspectives in post-colonial theory to defend Hindu-Christian dialogue about 'inclusivity'. Instead of adopting the Western 'objective' form of study, associated in India with colonial power, she commends instead a more engaged approach to shared forms of spirituality apparent among some Christians and Hindus living in India today.

The Catholic feminist Christian ethicist **Margaret Farley** also combines post-colonial theory, **liberation theology** and inter-faith dialogue in her engaged approach to Christian ethics. For example, in her 2002 book *Compassionate Respect* she defends the virtue of compassion within medical ethics.

In a 2009 essay she applies the concept of compassionate respect to the injustices in sub-Saharan Africa resulting from the AIDS pandemic. Prophetic discourse in this context, she argues, challenges colonial concepts of the 'world church' and involves energising and offering hope, calling for dialogue, specifying concrete ways to act and, especially, solidarity with, and engaging, those most affected. She defends the claim that prophets rightly articulate grief, cross borders of culture and faith and, in the context of AIDS, should be concerned with justice and truth in sexual relationships.

**Queer Christian ethics** has been particularly influenced by the radical Argentinian theologian **Marcella Althaus-Reid**. Her book *The Queer God* (2003) uses her extensive work among impoverished women in Brazil and elsewhere in Latin America 'to embrace God's part in the lives of gays, lesbians and the poor' and to develop a concept of holiness 'that overcomes sexual and colonial prejudices' (from the Preface). Although inspired by liberation theology, she comes to the conclusion that it tended to ignore people with alternative sexual preferences – hence her adoption of queer studies.

In 2009, the year that she died in Edinburgh, the North American Society of Christian Ethics established a study group entitled **LGBT and Queer Studies in Ethics**. Its aims are 'to define the conditions under which LGBT identities and relationships might be morally right, psychologically healthy, and socially constructive ... (and) to destabilize discourse in ethics by introducing queer concepts and methods to interrogate constructs of identity and sexuality'.

An important influence upon this study group has been the gradual introduction of gay marriage in Western countries and the opposition to this introduction by non-Western (and some Western) theologians. Chapter 6 will take this issue as an extended case-study.

**Ecological Christian ethics** is the topic explored in Chapter 4. **Animal ethics** has long been the major concern of the British theologian **Andrew Linzey**, the founder and director of the

Oxford Centre for Animal Ethics. In the 2018 collection *The Routledge Handbook of Religion and Animal Ethics*, edited by him and his wife Clair, a comprehensive agenda is set out for religious approaches to animal ethics.

Seven principles shape their work and passionate commitment:

- Good beyond the human.
- Relatedness to fellow beings.
- Experience of reverence for life.
- Intrinsic value of each sentient individual being.
- Sensitivity to animal suffering.
- Selfless living.
- Eschatological anticipation.

**David Clough**'s two-volume work *On Animals* (2012 and 2018) is equally passionate but more focused upon theology. He examines human exploitation of animals through the key Christian doctrines of creation, reconciliation and redemption.

**Disability Christian ethics** has been particularly stimulated by the influential American Christian ethicist **Stanley Hauerwas**, especially in his 1986 book *Suffering Presence*, and more recently by the Scottish pastoral theologian **John Swinton**, especially in his 2016 book *Becoming Friends of Time: Disability, Timefullness and Gentle Discipleship*.

In the final four chapters of *Suffering Presence*, Hauerwas offers a theological challenge to approaches to human disability that has influenced many other theologians writing in this area. By modern standards his use of the terms 'handicapped' and especially 'retarded' are now widely regarded as unacceptable. This apart, his chapter headings signal clearly the main direction of his approach: 'Suffering the Retarded: Should we prevent Retardation?'; 'The Moral Challenge of the Handicapped'; 'The Retarded, Society, and the Family: The Dilemma of Care'; and 'Community and Diversity: The Tyranny of Normality.'

For Hauerwas, writing from a perspective squarely based upon **virtue and character**: 'The issue is not whether retarded children can serve a public good, but whether we should be the kind of people, the kind of parents and community, that can receive, even welcome, them into our midst in a manner that allows them to flourish' (Hauerwas, 1986:167).

Swinton uses his former experience as a nurse and then as a hospital chaplain in three areas of neurological disability: those born with serious intellectual disability; those living with dementia; and those with acquired brain injury and personality change. He suggests that the most challenging group is the last, since the people affected are often very much aware of what they have lost and who they have now become. His overall aim is to challenge carers and cared-for alike to reconfigure time as God's time:

> This book might be conceived of as an extended meditation on what it means to live faithfully within the time that God has gifted to us. In the light of the experiences of people living with certain forms of neurological disability, the book seeks to offer a theological reimaging of the nature and purpose of time and in so doing offer some pointers for faithful living and the development of genuine communities of belonging (Swinton, 2016:11).

In a recent development, disability Christian ethics has been extended into the area of **sport. Nick J. Watson, Kevin Hargaden** and **Brian Brock**'s 2018 collection, *Theology, Disability and Sport: Social Justice Perspectives,* shows this clearly and has a particular focus upon the Special (or 'Para-') Olympics. They argue that the latter helps to correct distorted and less-than-Christian concepts of physical 'ability'.

In this collection Swinton argues that, within the Gospels, Jesus offers complex values-in-tension for a theology of sport: 'power and strength and weakness and vulnerability, competition and winning and Graciousness, defeat and lament, joy and brokenness … It may be that the greatest battle Christian sportswomen and men have to work through is how to love our neighbor when by defeating you, our neighbor seems to have just taken away our hopes and dreams' (Watson, Hargaden and Brock, 2018:80).

## FURTHER READING

All of the quotations of the following authors in this chapter can be found in greater detail in Section 1 of my *A Textbook of Christian Ethics*:

Abraham, Susan (2008), 'Postcolonial Theological Approaches to Hindu-Christian Studies,' in *Journal of Hindu-Christian Studies* (21:6, pp. 11–17). Fairly advanced level.

Aquinas, Thomas (1966), *Summa Theologica*, 1a2ae, 94, 4–6 (vol XXVIII of the English Dominican translation, London: Eyre & Spottiswoode, and New York: McGraw-Hill).

Copleston, F.C. (1976), *Aquinas* (New York: Harper & Row and Search, pp. 22–35). Fairly accessible.

Cupitt, Don (1971) *Christ and the Hiddenness of God* (London: SCM Press)

Cupitt, Don (1980) *Taking Leave of God* (London: SCM Press).

Fiorenza, Elisabeth Schüssler (1985), 'Women: Invisible in Church and Theology,' in *Concilium* (Edinburgh: T&T Clark, No. 182, pp. 6–12). Her many books include *In Memory of Her* (New York: Crossroad, 1983), *Discipleship of Equals* (New York: Crossroad, 1993) and *The Power of the Word* (Minneapolis, MN: Fortress, 2007). Not always very accessible.

Hare, John E. (1996) *The Moral Gap* (Oxford: Oxford University Press) A very important advanced-level book in the Oxford Studies in Theological Ethics series.

Horton, John & Mendus, Susan (eds) (1994), *After MacIntyre: Critical Perspectives on the Work of Alasdair MacIntyre* (Notre Dame, IN: University of Notre Dame Press) provides a very helpful critical guide to the debate generated by Alasdair MacIntyre, but it is at an advanced level.

Linzey, Andrew (1987), *Christianity and the Rights of Animals* (London: SPCK).

Linzey, Andrew (2009), *Why Animal Suffering Matters* (Oxford: Oxford University Press).

Luther, Martin (1966), *Treatise on Good Works* in *Luther's Works* (vol 44, Philadelphia: Fortress Press, trans. W.A. Lambert and Rev.JamesAtkinson, sections 4–6, 8, 12, 13–14 & 16). In this instance alone I have used the online translation of *The Project Gutenberg EBook*:https://www.gutenberg.org/files/418/418-h/418-h.htm (accessed 18/07/2019).

Porter, Jean (1995), *Moral Action and Christian Ethics* (New York and Cambridge: Cambridge University Press, pp. 182–188). This advanced-level book is part of New Studies in Christian Ethics.

## REFERENCES

Althaus-Reid, Marcella (2003), *The Queer God* (London: Routledge). Fairly advanced level.

Bonhoeffer, Dietrich (1955), *Ethics* (New York: Simon and Schuster, and London: SCM Press, 1978, pp. 3–6 & 9–13).

Bonhoeffer, Dietrich (1965), *No Rusty Swords* (New York: Harper and Row). Not always accessible.

Cahill, Lisa Sowle (2013), *Global Justice, Christology and Christian Ethics* (New York and Cambridge: Cambridge University Press). This is also part of New Studies in Christian Ethics and is of an advanced level.

Clough, David L. (2012 and 2018), *On Animals* (London: Bloomsbury T&T Clark). His well-received two volumes of systematic theology are at a more advanced level.

Cupitt, Don (1995), *Solar Ethics* (London: SCM Press, pp. 6–9, 13, 16, 19–20 & 45). Accessible.

Douglas, Kelly Brown (1994), *The Black Christ* (New York: Orbis). Accessible.

Farley, Margaret (2002), *Compassionate Respect: A Feminist Approach to Medical Ethics and Other Questions* (New York: Paulist Press). Accessible.

Fletcher, Joseph (1966), *Situation Ethics* (London: SCM Press, pp. 26–30, 30–33 & 37–39). Accessible.

Hare, John E. (2015), *God's Command* (Oxford: Oxford University Press). A very important advanced-level book in the Oxford Studies in Theological Ethics series.

Hauerwas, Stanley (1986), *Suffering Presence* (Notre Dame, IN: University of Notre Dame Press, and Edinburgh: T&T Clark, 1988). Generally accessible (more of his books will be listed in the References at the end of Chapters 2 and 3).

LGBT and Queer Studies in Ethics. Website can be found at: https://scethics. org/groups/lgbt-and-queer-studies-ethics (accessed 1/7/2019).

Linzey, Andrew & Linzey, Clair (eds) (2018), *The Routledge Handbook of Religion and Animal Ethics* (London: Routledge). Andrew Linzey's many books on animal ethics are typically accessible.

MacIntyre, Alasdair (1981), *After Virtue: A Study in Moral Theory* (London: Duckworth. Revised in 1985). This stunning book is well worth careful study.

Parsons, Susan Frank (1996), *Feminism and Christian Ethics* (Cambridge: Cambridge University Press). This is also part of New Studies in Christian Ethics series and is mostly accessible.

Pope John-Paul II (1993), *Veritatis Splendor* (London: Catholic Truth Society, sections 31–37, pp. 51–60).

Swinton, John (2016), *Becoming Friends of Time: Disability, Timefullness and Gentle Discipleship* (London: SCM Press). Fairly accessible.

Watson, Nick J., Hargaden, Kevin & Brock, Brian (eds) (2018), *Theology, Disability and Sport: Social Justice Perspectives* (London: Routledge). Some essays are more accessible than others.

# POLITICS, ECONOMICS AND SOCIAL JUSTICE

Within the early church there is one theologian who stands head and shoulders above others in addressing the crucial question of how church and state – Christianity and the political order –should be related. Under considerable pressure, both from within his church and from society at large, Augustine wrestled with this issue at great length and established criteria that have continued to shape Western societies. The influence of his thought has been immense.

## AUGUSTINE OF HIPPO

The theologian, polemicist and polymath **Augustine** (c. 354–430), Bishop of Hippo in North Africa, is not to be confused with Augustine, the first Archbishop of Canterbury, who arrived in Kent as a missionary sent from Rome in 597.

Augustine's mother was a devout Catholic Christian but his father was not. He wrestled with this division between his parents as a young man, exploring the dualistic teaching of Manichaeism (with its strong sense of the world being sharply divided by competing good and evil forces) and studying, and then teaching, rhetoric and logic at university. He was finally baptised as a Catholic Christian at the age of 33, having been particularly influenced by Ambrose, Bishop of Milan. He was soon ordained as a priest and then became Bishop of Hippo in 396. He remained there as bishop, at a time of considerable political turmoil, until his death.

Augustine wrote his monumental work, *The City of God*, in order to counter the accusation that Christianity, adopted as the official religion by the Roman Emperor Constantine earlier in the

4th century, had weakened the Empire. Specifically, he developed the notion of 'the two cities' – the earthly city and the heavenly city – to explain why this was not so.

He insisted there were points of contact between the two cities and, as a result, the Christian could be a good citizen. However, the two cities were not identical and finally the Christian is a 'pilgrim' in the earthly city on a journey to the heavenly city: 'There is, in fact, one city of people who choose to live by the standard of the flesh, another of those who choose to live by the standard of the spirit.'

## AUGUSTINE: THE EARTHLY AND HEAVENLY CITIES

Book XIV in the final section of *The City of God* (written in the period 420–426) gives a particularly clear and mature account of Augustine's notion of the two cities.

From the earthly city people may have enjoyment of earthly, temporal peace for body and soul, whereas from the heavenly city they may have enjoyment of eternal peace. Irrational animals, in contrast, are concerned only with satisfying their appetites and avoiding pain and, thus, having bodily peace.

Human beings, unlike animals, have a rational soul and can engage in deliberate thought and organise their lives according to ethical standards. Yet, given their weakness, they need divine direction and assistance to meet these standards. While they live in mortal bodies, they are pilgrims in a foreign land, walking by faith and not by sight, in subjection to immortal God.

This subjection is based upon two chief precepts – love of God and love of neighbour – with, for Augustine, three objects of this love – God, themselves and their neighbours. In so far as this love is possible, people will have peace and ordered harmony.

For a man, the love of neighbour especially includes his wife, his children and members of his household. All of these are his responsibility 'both in the order of nature and in the framework of human society'. This is where domestic peace starts and it involves wives obeying husbands, children obeying their parents, and servants obeying their masters. Yet, in terms of the heavenly city, 'even those who give orders are the servants of those whom they appear to command'. In these terms, their 'orders' derive not from a 'lust for domination' but from 'a dutiful concern for the interests of others' and from compassion.

In Genesis, Augustine argues, it can be seen that God created human beings to have dominion not over other human beings but only over irrational animals. That precept even applies to slaves until the time of Noah. It was only because of sin after Noah that slavery (and war) came into existence, with human beings subjected to bondage. Slavery is a punishment from God for sin and is now an unchangeable part of the order of nature.

If slaves cannot be set free by their masters, then slaves 'may make slavery, in a sense, free, by serving not with slyness of fear, but with the fidelity of affection, until all injustice disappears and all human lordship and power is annihilated, and God is all in all'.

Even though slavery is part of the order of nature, Augustine still argues that slaves should be allowed to worship and should be treated with equal affection as members of a household. The householder should be concerned about the worship and service of God among all in his household, 'longing and praying that they may come to the heavenly home'. However, until they reach that home, it is the duty of slaves 'to put up with their condition as servants'.

Domestic peace contributes to the peace of the earthly city. This peace is important even for the pilgrim on the path to the heavenly city. However, when a household is based upon faith it 'looks forward to the blessings which are promised as eternal in the future'. The earthly city, whose life is not based upon this faith, aims at earthly peace based upon 'a kind of compromise between human wills about the things relevant to mortal life'. The heavenly city does need this form of peace and 'does not hesitate to obey the laws of the earthly city', which are designed for regulating mortal life, *but* it 'knows only one God as the object of worship and decrees'.

So any laws based upon beliefs in other gods must be rejected. The heavenly city can support a variety of earthly laws, customs or institutions 'provided that no hindrance is presented thereby to the religion which teaches the one supreme and true God is to be worshipped'. Indeed, more than that, the heavenly city on its earthly pilgrimage contributes significantly to the peace and social life of the earthly city.

## STRENGTHS

With his notion of the two cities (which are more modes of existence than places) Augustine depicts an important tension within Christian ethics between the 'now' and the 'not yet'. Within the first three Gospels this tension is typically depicted in the words of Jesus by the notion of the 'Kingdom of Heaven' or 'Kingdom of God' (terms which are used interchangeably). The 'kingdom' here is also not exactly a place. It signifies God's guiding presence within the everyday world and God's future presence beyond the world: the 'now' and the 'not yet'.

Augustine's depiction of the life of faith as a form of pilgrimage also has considerable resonance for Christian ethics. The person of faith is seen to be within the world but not entirely conformed to the world. The earthly city can give pilgrims a context of peace and order but that, in itself, is not the main objective of pilgrimage. Pilgrims finally have their sight on the heavenly city.

In terms of the love commands, people of faith can know something about love of God and love of neighbour (and, significantly, Augustine adds to this love of self) within the earthly city. However, at best, this is partial knowledge of love. A full expression of love is only to be found in the heavenly city.

In addition, it is evident that Augustine, despite a strong emphasis upon human frailty and sin, accepts some notion of natural law and order. For him it is natural for households, with reciprocal duties for those within them to each other, to be ordered and harmonious. On a much larger scale it is also natural for cities to be ordered and harmonious.

Again, subjecting people to slavery is not seen as being originally part of the natural order. Even though slavery now needs to be accepted as part of that order, it (like war) is a consequence of sin and human disobedience. In terms of faith, slaves must be treated equally alongside other members of a household. At most, Augustine is offering a very reluctant acceptance of slavery (and war) in a sinful world.

Finally, Augustine sees the need for civil laws and customs. They are an essential part of a harmonious society. He emphatically is not advocating lawlessness. In his view it is only when laws and customs militate against the worship of God that they must be rejected.

So, against his critics, he is able to claim that Christian faith can strengthen rather than weaken (appropriate) civil order. In short, people of faith can be good citizens, even though they are still (temporary) pilgrims on the path to the heavenly city.

## WEAKNESSES

To the modern mind there are, perhaps unsurprisingly, some very obvious weaknesses in Augustine's position.

His failure to condemn slavery is a clear example of weakness for many people today. Here he echoes the instructions in Ephesians:

> Slaves, obey your earthly masters with fear and trembling, in single-ness of heart, as you obey Christ; not only while being watched, and in order to please them, but as slaves of Christ, doing the will of God from the heart. Render service with enthusiasm, as to the Lord and not to men and women, knowing that whatever good we do, we will receive the same again from the Lord, whether we are slaves or free. And, masters, do the same to them. Stop threatening them, for you know that both of you have the same Master in heaven, and with him there is no partiality (Eph. 6.5–9).

With the benefit of hindsight it is often pointed out that the New Testament – and Augustine following the New Testament – never actually condemns slavery. The Greek word for 'slave' is used descriptively and metaphorically in the New Testament rather than judgmentally. Augustine does add significantly to this by identifying slavery with sin, but he still sees it as part of the present natural order that must not be transgressed.

One way to modify this difficulty is to argue that 'slavery' in the Roman world is not to be confused with the brutal mass transportation of black Africans to work as slaves in the Caribbean sugar plantations in the 18th century. Perhaps not, but Roman slavery was hardly civilised by 21st century ethical standards. Post-colonial and womanist Christian ethicists are unlikely to be impressed by this particular argument. It *was* still involuntary servitude and subjugation enforced by a colonial power.

In addition, there are obvious signs of patriarchy in Augustine's depiction of household duties (again following Ephesians). Within the household the man is clearly master, even though as a person of faith he is finally subject to God. It is the man who must ensure the spiritual welfare of others within the household and it is to the man that all others in the household must be obedient.

Finally, animals do not fare well. Augustine regards animals as 'irrational' and has no qualms about human dominance over them. It will be seen in Chapter 4 that **Thomas Aquinas** follows Augustine here and even produces a gender-based hierarchy of rationality – husbands, wives, slaves and then animals, in that order. Feminist and ecological Christian ethicists alike are seldom impressed by either Augustine or Aquinas at this point.

## AQUINAS: ON PRINCELY GOVERNMENT

Aquinas's mature work, *De Regimine Principum* ('On the Rule of Princes'), sets out clearly his understanding of the relationship between church and state. It has few of the caveats of Augustine's notion of two cities. Unsurprisingly there is no longer a fear that the Christian risks worshipping other gods by being too close to the state. Nor is it necessary for Aquinas to emphasise that the Christian is a passing pilgrim.

Church and state now work hand-in-hand within a single entity. Pope and king/prince are both parts of the same Catholic Church, albeit with the king subject to the pope on spiritual matters. Within 13th century Europe the Catholic Church is by now the Universal Church. This, emphatically, is Christendom.

Aquinas looks to nature to deduce the duties of a king. For him a universal principle within nature is that all things find their place under the direction of God. A particular principle is that rational human beings mirror this divine control. Human beings are social by nature and live in community. The duty of the king is to control this community with intelligence. Aquinas argues that, in a somewhat similar way, bees also have a ruler – albeit with the difference that their behaviour derives from instinct rather than from intelligence.

God's control involves both the creation of the world and its continuing governance. Similarly, the rational human soul gives initial form to the body and controls ongoing bodily movement. Likewise with kings: only some kings establish cities, but all kings have a duty to govern their city whether they established it or not. It is the duty of kings to protect all that they govern.

When establishing a city it is the duty of a king to choose a suitable site to ensure the health of the inhabitants, their security from being attacked, and that they have sufficient physical sustenance, housing, organisation and churches. 'Such, very briefly, are the points a king must consider when establishing a city or a kingdom, and they can all be arrived at by analogy with the creation of the world.'

Aquinas reminds the reader at this point that, while human beings need all of these provisions, they also have a destiny after this mortal life – namely the 'final blessedness and enjoyment of God' after death. If the final destiny were thought simply to be bodily health, then doctors would govern. If it were abundant riches, then economists would govern, and, if knowledge of truth, then professors would govern.

'But the object for which a community is gathered together is to live a virtuous life ... not merely to live in virtue, but rather through virtuous life to attain to the enjoyment of God.' And this can only be attained through divine grace: 'The ministry of this kingdom is entrusted not to the rulers of the earth but to priests, so that temporal affairs may remain distinct from those spiritual: and, in particular, to the High Priest, the successor of Peter and Vicar of Christ [i.e., the pope].'

So the king is 'the supreme power in temporal things' but it is the pope who is supreme in spiritual things. Unambiguously Aquinas asserts that, 'under Christ's Law, kings must be subject to priests':

> For this reason, it came about by the admirable dispensation of divine providence, that in the city of Rome which God chose to be the main centre of Christendom, it gradually became the custom for the rulers of the city to be subject to the pontiffs.

## STRENGTHS

There is a strong sense of priorities in this passage. From the perspective of Christian ethics, life in the presence of God takes priority over everything else. In the teaching of Jesus within the first three Gospels, once again, it is the Kingdom of God/Heaven that takes priority in parable after parable. If someone really believes in the reality of a personal God and the reality of God's presence within human life present and future, everything else pales into insignificance.

Within the assumptions of medieval Christendom it also follows that rulers, and even monarchs, are finally subject to God's command mediated through the church. Priests and, especially, popes are custodians of God's commands and, as a result, should expect everyone (however mighty) to be subject to them.

There is also a very clear use of natural law in this passage. Aquinas draws from nature – animal nature as well as human nature – to claim that an ordered society does need an authoritative, hierarchical leadership. Without such leadership there could be social chaos.

If Augustine's vision of the two cities is fraught with ambiguity, Aquinas's vision of medieval Christendom and Princely Government subject finally to God's command appears to represent order and harmony. Grace crowns natural order.


## WEAKNESSES

And yet, to modern eyes, the weaknesses and potential for serious abuse of Aquinas's position here are obvious. To take the 'strengths' in reverse order:

Within many democratic societies today there is much suspicion about the assumption that an ordered society does need an authoritative, hierarchical leadership. It was this assumption that gave popular support to Hitler within pre-war Germany, to Stalin within the pre-war Soviet Union and to Mao Zedong during the Cultural Revolution in China. And, as a result, millions of people in the 20th century perished.

To modern eyes, Aquinas also shows his limitations by supposing that a powerful monarchy is 'natural' in the sense that analogies from nature can give it ethical support. It will be obvious to most Western people in the 21st century that monarchy can only survive today in the West if it becomes purely symbolic, bereft of serious political power. This is now the case within the handful of European countries where constitutional monarchy still survives.

In addition, few would resort to natural law theory to support constitutional monarchy – or even, as it happens, democracy. For most people it is largely irrelevant whether or not democracy is 'natural' in the sense that it is to be found in nature (this would be very difficult to demonstrate). Democracy is usually accepted because it is 'fair' and 'accountable', rather than because it is 'natural'.

Second, many today might be sceptical about the assumption that priests and, especially, popes are custodians of God's commands and, as a result, should expect everyone (however mighty) to be subject to them. With reports of scandals about the clerical abuse of minors being so widespread today, it would be very difficult to defend this assumption. Many might argue, instead, that all human institutions (including churches) should be subject to independent, judicial arbitration and unfettered media scrutiny. In short, they too should be accountable.

Third, while many people of faith might agree with the precept that life in the presence of God takes priority over everything else, there is an important question to raise about whether such a precept should be imposed rather than freely chosen. At a time of religiously inspired violence, this question is crucial. It is one thing to make this claim for oneself but quite another to seek to impose it upon others.

In this respect Aquinas (and Augustine before him) lapsed badly. Aquinas came to the following conclusion in *Summa Theologica* (II.11): 'if it be just that forgers and other malefactors are put to death without mercy by the secular authority, with how much greater reason may heretics not only be excommunicated, but also put to death, when once they are convicted of heresy.' Augustine, towards the end of his life, also sought state help to suppress the Donatists, whom he regarded as 'heretics'. As with militant Islamists today, a combination of power and strongly held religious beliefs can be very dangerous.

Chapter 7 will return to this issue when considering the attitudes to Jewish people of Aquinas and, especially, **Martin Luther**.

## LUTHER: TRADE AND USURY

If Aquinas sought to endorse the order and harmony of European Christendom, the Reformation inspired by Luther seriously fractured it. Luther's critique of the papacy, especially, put a serious question mark against the central precept of Christendom. Far from being a guardian of God's commands, the pope was criticised, in effect, for being an agent of deep corruption. People were now encouraged to read the Bible for themselves and to let that instruct their individual consciences, unmediated by popes and priests, in order to discern Christian faith.

Luther began work leading to the treatise *Trade and Usury* in 1520, the year that he was excommunicated by Pope Leo, and he completed it four years later. Inevitably this was a time of considerable ferment for Luther, working through the theological and practical implications of his bold rebellion.

Luther is no economist. His assumptions about economics and, especially, about 'usury' are still medieval. Like many others at the time, he shares Aristotle's precept that money does not produce money – hence his rejection of usury (i.e., money lent at what he deems to be excessive interest rates). He also rejects greed, quoting 1 Timothy 6.9–10:

> But those who want to be rich fall into temptation and are trapped by many senseless and harmful desires that plunge people into ruin and destruction. For the love of money is a root of all kinds of evil, and in their eagerness to be rich some have wandered away from the faith and pierced themselves with many pains.

It is his use of the Bible to address the propriety of trade that is highly indicative for Christian ethics. In contrast to more radical evangelical preachers at the time, Luther makes a determined effort to discern biblically justified ways that commercial trade might be undertaken.

He admits at the outset that trade, in the form of buying and selling, is necessary and that the patriarchs in the Old Testament bought and sold animal products. Yet he is critical of foreign trade for luxury items, such as silk, gold and spices, 'which minister only to ostentation but serve no useful purpose, and which drain away the money of land and people'.

He is also highly critical of trade that involves what he regards as excessive profits or personal debt – two key features of capitalist economies today. With his characteristic pungency he writes: 'When once the rogue's eye and greedy belly of a merchant find that people must have his wares, or that the buyer is poor and needs them, he takes advantage of him and raises the price.' In short, the merchants sell their goods as expensively as they can and exploit the needy. Instead they should be asking what is 'right and fair'.

But how do merchants establish what is right and fair? Luther admits that there are problems here. Some goods require expensive transport or may be scarce due to weather conditions. His maxim is that merchants do need to cover their costs and be compensated for their labour and risk. However, it would be best if 'the temporal authorities appoint in this matter wise and honest men to compute the costs of all sorts of wares and accordingly set prices'.

In other words, Luther opts for regulated price fixing rather than free trade. Yet the realist in him quickly realises that this is not likely to happen, even in the 16th century (although it was imposed disastrously by Stalin in the 20th century Soviet Union). So, in the absence of regulated price fixing, he places the burden on 'your conscience to be careful not to overcharge your neighbour, and to seek a modest living, not the goals of greed'.

He now suggests four specifically Christian ways of 'exchanging external goods with others' that do not involve greed, unwarranted profits or debt:

The first two are drawn from Mathew's Sermon on the Mount:

> If anyone wants to sue you and take your coat, give your cloak as well; and if anyone forces you to go one mile, go also the second mile. Give to everyone who begs from you, and do not refuse anyone who wants to borrow from you (5.40–42).

From this Luther draws the conclusion that Christians can either let others steal their property or they can voluntarily give their property away to the needy. Perhaps tongue in cheek, he admits that, while this is 'lofty Christian work', it will not find favour with merchants and will result in less trade.

The third way he draws from Luke 6.35: 'love your enemies, do good, and lend, expecting nothing in return.' So, rather than giving away their property to the needy, Christians can lend it to them instead. Again, Luther admits that this is 'lofty' Christian work since this form of lending takes the risk – given that it must expect nothing in return – of becoming simply a gift.

The problems here for merchants are obvious, but Luther reminds his readers that 'Christians are rare people on earth'. Borrowing would be fine among these rare people. Christians who borrow would willingly return what they had been lent and Christian lenders would be willing to forgo repayment from a Christian borrower who was simply unable to repay. However, when people 'are not Christians, the temporal authorities ought to compel them to repay what they have borrowed'.

The fourth and final way, Luther suggests, is just to have a cash or exchange economy without any credit or debt being involved: 'if only hard cash or wares on hand were exchanged in trade, the greatest and most harmful dangers and faults and failing of trade and commerce would be well out of the way ... many a man would have to maintain his humble status and be content with a modest living.'

## STRENGTHS

Luther is well aware that he is offering 'lofty' advice here. Positively, this can be seen as a counsel of perfection, similar to the command in the Sermon on the Mount to love your enemies and to pray for those who persecute you – with its impossible conclusion that followers should 'be perfect, therefore, as your heavenly Father is perfect' (Matthew 5.48). A counsel of perfection is, at most, attainable partially, rarely and only by exceptional individuals. Most Christians are not exceptional, which is why they regard those few who are as saints.

A counsel of perfection does have a proper role in Christian ethics. For example, if everyone were to abide by the simple principle that lying is always wrong then it can be seen that much of the judicial system would not be needed. We would be able to trust each other always to tell the truth. We would still have disputes when interests clashed, but these too could be resolved more readily in a thoroughly truthful society.

Such a counsel of perfection does not need to claim that there ever has been such a society. It needs only to speculate about would happen *if* there ever were to be such a society. Perhaps that is what Luther is doing here. He is speculating about what trade would look like *if* everyone really was a Christian.

He is also making a very honest attempt to address an extremely complex set of issues that still divides professional economists today. The latter remain divided, for example, on the extent that markets should be free and unregulated and on the merits, or demerits, of command economies.

Luther even seems to recognise frankly that his proposals are unlikely to convince merchants themselves (on whom he and everyone else depends). There is a commendable hesitancy apparent in his approach to the issue of trading.

Finally, and crucially, he goes to some length to explore the biblical base for (most of) his proposals. In the absence of papal authority, he is determined to heed the authority of the Bible and to show readers exactly how he does this. He does appeal to individual conscience (and occasionally to popular proverbs) but not usually before he has already appealed to the Bible.

WEAKNESSES

The most obvious weakness is in his fourth Christian way of trading, namely simply to have a cash or exchange economy without any credit or debt being involved. It is at this point that he shows himself to be medieval in his thinking. He shows none of the economic sophistication of the Dominican theologian and economist **Albino Barrera**, who has contributed so significantly to *New Studies in Christian Ethics*.

Even in terms of early 16th century Europe, national economies could no longer function on the basis of cash or exchange. The idea would have been economically ridiculous even then. This is not just 'lofty' thinking but hopelessly impracticable thinking. As admirable as it might at first seem in ethical terms, eliminating credit and national debt and returning to cash rather than notional money (or, even more primitively, to exchanging goods) would have wrecked European countries in the 16th century, let alone in the 21st century.

In addition, it is noticeable that Luther does not justify this fourth way biblically in the manner that he does for the other three ways. Judged by his own standards, this does appear to be a lapse.

Looking at his suggestions as a whole, it is clear that Luther, unlike Aquinas, has considerable affinity with Augustine's notion of Christians being pilgrims on a path to the heavenly city in an alien land, itself committed only to the earthly city. Whereas Augustine writes about two cities, Luther writes elsewhere about two kingdoms. So in a treatise written a year earlier, *Temporal Authority*, he says:

> All who are not Christians belong to the kingdom of the world and are under the law. There are few true believers, and still fewer who live the Christian life, who do not resist evil and indeed themselves do no evil. For this reason God has provided for them a different government beyond the Christian estate and kingdom of God. He has subjected them to the sword (para. 90).

When applied to trade, this dual kingdom notion appears to result in a double-standard – especially his judgment that, when people 'are not Christians, the temporal authorities ought to compel them to repay what they have borrowed'. So, if a borrower is not a Christian, it might be considered appropriate for a Christian lender to resort to the civil authorities to get the loan returned (unless the Christian lender choses to be magnanimous). Whereas, if both the borrower and the lender are Christians, this would not be appropriate.

In short, one rule for the Christian borrower and another rule for the non-Christian borrower.

There is also a danger that, despite its commendable features, a counsel of perfection in Luther's hands might promote a highly exclusive understanding of what it is to be a Christian. Indeed, his claim that 'Christians are rare people on earth' might be seen to promote exclusivity, especially if he assumes that he is also one those rare people.

## TWO KINGDOMS OR ONE KINGDOM?

Aquinas and Luther present a stark contrast here in drawing upon different features of Augustine's *City of God*. Aquinas extends Augustine's use of natural law but he writes at a time when Christians are by now not remotely a beleaguered minority. Church and state are meant to work harmoniously together and Christians are no longer pilgrims in an alien land. Luther, in contrast, extends Augustine's notion of the two cities so that they become two whole kingdoms. Beleaguered and scarce Christians are now, once again, just temporary pilgrims.

Seen in these terms, Christian ethics today might be mapped along these two very different trajectories – One Kingdom or Two Kingdoms; two contrasting ways of viewing Christian life in society. Of course, this is not the only way that Christian ethics can be mapped historically. Yet it can illuminate a crucial tension within Christian ethics today, namely how it should relate to a self-consciously pluralistic society.

## TWO KINGDOMS

Very soon a tension emerges between Martin Luther and **John Calvin** (1509–1564) on this key issue. Both of these key Reformers agree that civil government is essential for the good of society, that governments are appointed by God and that they are, therefore, to be obeyed by individual citizens.

Specifically, in his *Commentary on the Epistle to the Romans*, Calvin concludes that:

> The reason why we ought to be subject to magistrates is because they are constituted by God's ordination. For since it pleases God thus to govern the world, he who attempts to invert the order of God, and thus to resist God himself, despises his power; since to despise the providence of him who is the founder of civil power is to carry on war with him.

Luther might largely agree with this.

But what should Christians do if these civil authorities give them an order that runs contrary to Christian faith? Here Calvin introduces something different. In his *Commentary on Daniel* he advises:

> Earthly princes lay aside all their power when they rise up against God, and are unworthy of being reckoned in the number of human-kind. We ought rather utterly to defy them than to obey them whenever they are restive and wish to spoil God of his rights, and, as it were, to seize upon his throne and draw him down from heaven.

With the rise to power of Hitler in the 1930s both of the Reformed theologians **Karl Barth** (1885–1968) and **Dietrich Bonhoeffer** (1906–1945) were confronted sharply with this dilemma. Barth responds by returning from Germany to his native Switzerland and, as already seen, Bonhoeffer responds by returning from the United States to his native Germany. Both become firm opponents of Hitler, despite his being 'constituted by God's ordination', but Bonhoeffer takes this opposition considerably further by actually joining the unsuccessful bomb plot to assassinate Hitler.

In his seminal 1929 theological commentary *The Epistle to the Romans*, Barth argues firmly against political revolution. Writing 12 years after the Russian Revolution, he identifies the problem with the revolutionary as follows:

> He forgets that he is not the One, that he is not the subject of the freedom which he so earnestly desires, that, for all the strange brightness of his eyes, he is not the Christ who stands before the Grand Inquisitor, but is, contrariwise, the Grand Inquisitor encountered by the Christ (Barth, 1929: on Rms. 12.1).

Barth considers the command in Romans 13.1: 'Let every person be subject to the governing authorities; for there is no authority except from God, and those authorities that exist have been instituted by God.' And from this he argues that, if an authority is evil, this 'means to withdraw and make way; it means to have no resentment and not to overthrow' (Barth, 1929: on Rms. 13.1). By withdrawing to Switzerland when confronted with Hitler, this is exactly what Barth does.

The Russian Orthodox mystic **Nicolas Berdyaev** (1874–1948) followed a similar path to Barth, albeit from a very different theological perspective. In his 1927 book *Freedom and the Spirit*, written five years after his expulsion from revolutionary Russia, he makes a sharp contrast between mass religion/ideology and 'truly spiritual individuals whose lives are directed towards the highest aims'. It is evident that he identifies with the latter:

> Saints, prophets, geniuses, men, in short, who live on the higher planes of the spiritual life and who are capable of authentic creation, have no need of monarchy or republicanism, conservatism or

revolution, nor yet of constitutions and educational establishments. For the aristocracy of the spirit does not bear the burden of history for itself. On the contrary it is made to submit to institutions, reforms, and systems whether old or new, in the name of the so-called people and of the collective, or, in other words, of the happiness of the average man (Berdyaev, 1935: xi–xii).

Bonhoeffer, despite being steeped in Barth and Luther and despite his youthful pacifism, does exactly the opposite to Barth and Berdyaev. Remarkably he returns, opposes, joins an assassination plot and, finally, is executed.

Would the German–American theologian **Reinhold Niebuhr** have reacted in the same way to Hitler had he been born in Germany? As a colleague of Bonhoeffer in the United States he was party to his decision to return to Germany, but, unlike Bonhoeffer, his approach to Christian ethics is more distant from that of Barth. He is a champion of what is now termed **realist ethics** by Christian ethicists such as his most eminent modern interpreter **Robin Lovin**.

In his politically influential 1932 book *Moral Man and Immoral Society*, Niebuhr (1892–1971) argues, with echoes of Berdyaev, that there is an ethical chasm between the behaviour expected of an individual and that expected of society at large:

> From the perspective of society the highest moral ideal is justice. From the perspective of the individual the highest ideal is unselfishness. Society must strive for justice even if it is forced to use means, such as self-assertion, resistance, coercion and perhaps resentment, which cannot gain the moral sanction of the most sensitive moral spirit. The individual must strive to realise his life by losing and finding himself in something greater than himself (Niebuhr, 1960: 257).

For Niebuhr these two ethical perspectives are not easily harmonised. Niebuhr is particularly impatient with utopian ethical stances, including the pacifism that characterised Bonhoeffer's youth. For him it is a deep confusion to imagine that society can behave ethically in a way that an individual might. Indeed, 'whenever religious idealism brings forth its purest fruits and places the strongest check upon selfish desire, it results in policies which, from the political perspective, are quite impossible' (Niebuhr, 1960: 270).

Instead, he believes, we need to make a clear distinction between ethical judgments applied to the self and to others and ethical judgments applied to social and political groups. Individual idealists may inspire other people but, unless their number grows large, they cannot expect to affect the policy of government.

The outcome of Niebuhr's analysis is considerably to modify Luther's Two Kingdoms notion. It is not simply that there are two kingdoms – one temporal and the other eternal – that are in an uneasy relationship. It is rather that all individuals (whether they are Christian or not) are likely to be in tension with political realities.

This does not stop Niebuhr himself from being politically active throughout his career (much more so than Berdyaev), but it does modify what he expects a Christian (or any other idealist) to achieve in the political realm. Arguably, though, it also lets cynically minded politicians off any ethical hook.

Writing today, **Stanley Hauerwas** is a sharp critic of Niebuhr's realist position within Christian ethics and champions, instead, a more Barthian **witness ethics**.

In his first book, the 1974 *Vision and Virtue*, Hauerwas's style of Christian ethics is focused mainly upon the individual Christian. Taking a cue from the novelist and philosopher Iris Murdoch he argues that ethics is about 'seeing' things differently. A decade later, however, in his 1983 book *The Peaceable Kingdom* (which will be considered in Chapter 3) his focus is upon the Christian community.

Hauerwas's most widely read book is the 1989 populist *Resident Aliens: Life in the Christian Colony* (co-written with William Willimon). Here Christian pastors are told:

> If we live as a colony of resident aliens within a hostile environment, which, in the most subtle but deadly of ways, corrupts and co-opts us as Christians, then the pastor is called to help us gather the resources we need to be the colony of God's righteousness (Hauerwas & Willimon, 1989:139–140).

In short, Hauerwas's position within Christian ethics has by now adopted a sharp Two Kingdoms perspective. He writes as an American, so the metaphor of 'resident aliens' refers to immigrants working in America who have not yet gained full citizenship – not to creatures from outer-space, as it might more readily by under-stood by Europeans. Emphatically it is a Two Kingdoms metaphor.

Hauerwas has been accused repeatedly of sectarianism for using this metaphor. Whether fair or not, this criticism has persuaded him to adopt, instead, the biblical term 'witness' (*martus* in Greek) in his most recent books. Nevertheless, he still differentiates Christian witnesses sharply from society at large. They remain pilgrims in a sinful world.

Writing as a Catholic, the Mexican liberation theologian **José Porfirio Miranda** (1924–2001) might also be seen, perhaps surprisingly, as an exponent of a Two Kingdoms approach to Christian ethics.

In his 1977 book *Marx and the Bible* Miranda explicitly con-demns differentiating ownership and wealth that makes some rich and some poor within the same society. He argues at length that an acceptance of such wealth by Christians is a distortion of biblical and early church teaching.

For him this distortion has been aided by translations of the Hebrew word for 'righteousness' (*tsedaka*) in the Bible as 'almsgiv-ing'. *Tsedaka*, he argues, is not meant to be a term for voluntary charity. It is meant to signify handing over to others what properly belongs to them – it is simply an act of redressing an injustice. He also takes literally sayings of Jesus such as Luke 6.24: 'Alas for you who are rich.'

As the title of his book indicates, there is a strong mixture of biblical and Marxist terms in Miranda's condemnation of differ-entiating wealth:

> The fact that differentiating wealth is un-acquirable without violence and spoliation is presupposed by the Bible in its pointed anathemas against the rich; therefore almsgiving is nothing more than restitution of what has been stolen, and thus the Bible calls it justice (Miranda, 1977:19–20).

He makes an emphatic demand that 'the time has come for Christianity to break a long chain of hypocrisy and collusion with the established powers'. At this point Miranda does seem to be a Two Kingdoms exponent.

Ironically, Miranda's nemesis, exponents of the so-called **prosperity gospel**, have followed a similar path. **Kate Bowler**'s well-received 2013 book, *Blessed: A History of the American Prosperity Gospel*, traces the long history of this broad populist movement in the United States and beyond into the global South. She concludes that the key premise of the movement is that 'the virtuous would be richly compensated while the wicked would eventually stumble ... a theology of excess that separated the faith-filled few from the poverty of the masses' (Bowler, 2013:226).

## ONE KINGDOM

In contrast, One Kingdom approaches to Christian ethics typically do not differentiate Christians from non-Christians so sharply. Using one form or another of natural law theory, they are more inclined to see continuities between ethics in general and Christian ethics in particular.

The term 'Christendom', although still championed by some proponents of **radical orthodoxy**, is not popular today. Viewed in terms of the hegemony of the 13th century European Catholic Church, which Aquinas inhabited, Christendom hardly exists anywhere in the world today. The less-specific term One Kingdom will be used here, instead, to denote an approach to Christian ethics that sees continuities, rather than sharp discontinuities, between church and society.

A former Anglican Archbishop of Canterbury, **William Temple** (1881–1944), is a clear 20th century example of the One Kingdom approach. In his small, popular 1941 book, *Christianity and Social Order*, he sets out his understanding of church and society in war-time Britain. He summarises his main argument succinctly:

> Freedom, Fellowship, Service – these are the three principles of a Christian social order, derived from the still more fundamental Christian postulates that Man is a child of God and is destined for a life of eternal fellowship with Him (Temple, 1976:77).

At the outset he emphasises that these three principles, on their own, will not resolve social issues such as unemployment. Technical knowledge, for example about economics, will also be needed to achieve that. However, the principles should guide political decision-makers. These principles might also persuade politicians that unemployment in peacetime is a sign of a diseased society that, in ethical terms, *does* need to be remedied.

For Temple the primary principle of Christian ethics and Christian politics is 'respect for every person simply as a person', with everyone seen as a child of God. He insists that 'there is in each a worth absolutely independent of all usefulness to society' (Temple, 1976:69–70). It is from this principle that he then derives the three general principles of freedom, fellowship and service.

Freedom, for him, is not simply an absence of compulsion; it is also (more positively) freedom as self-control, self-determination and self-direction. He argues that revolutionary politics, despite its own rhetoric, tends to suppress such freedom.

Fellowship, for him, takes seriously the social nature of human beings. It also sees that freedom for individuals 'exists for the most part in and through those intermediate groups' such as family, church congregation, trade union and school.

The combination of freedom and fellowship then 'issues in the obligation of service' – both voluntary service within the community and service at work. Hence the triumvirate of freedom, fellowship and service.

So, unlike Barth, Temple derives his principles partly from theological considerations and partly from his understanding of human nature. He also assumes that human nature, although prone to sin, is 'not merely bad' and that humanity is 'naturally and incurably social'. This is much more akin to Aquinas than to Luther.

An approach very similar to Temple's can be found in many recent papal encyclicals. It is, for example, very evident in Pope John-Paul II's 1993 encyclical *Veritatis Splendor* (mentioned in Chapter 1). It is also evident in **Pope John XXIII**'s seminal 1963 encyclical *Pacem in Terris* (Peace on Earth).

Yet there is also an important conceptual difference between Temple and John XXIII. Temple uses the concept of principles, itemising freedom, fellowship and service; John XXIII uses the reciprocal concepts of mutual rights and duties. For him, rights consist of truth, justice, friendship and respect for freedom and derive from natural law. On this understanding, 'service' would be a reciprocal duty or obligation as it is a commitment 'to promote the common good of all'.

A crucial watershed between Temple's *Christianity and Social Order* and John XXIII's *Pacem in Terris* is the establishment of the United Nations Organisation in 1945 (a year after Temple's death) and its formal approval of the Universal Declaration of Human Rights in 1949. By 1963 the pope is explicitly using the language of human rights, albeit emphasising the concept of reciprocal duties or obligations and the concept of the common good – concepts drawn from contemporary Catholic social ethics.

John XXIII summarises his position in this way:

> We have established that states have the right to exist, to prosper, to acquire the aids necessary for their development and to rely principally on their own efforts in so doing. They have the right also to protect their reputation and to insist on due honours being paid to them. It follows logically that there is a corresponding obligation on all of them to see that every one of these rights is safeguarded and that nothing is done to violate them (Pope John XXIII, 1980: para. 92).

If all states, he argues, are to have these reciprocal rights and obligations upheld and respected, then 'some sort of world government' is required:

> Such a world government, enjoying an authority extending to the farthest corners of the earth and having in its service agencies capable of advancing the universal common good, will need to come into being through universal consent and not be imposed by force (Pope John XXIII, 1980: para. 138).

Although he is well aware of criticisms of both the United Nations and its 1949 declaration, he hopes that it will go 'from strength to strength, perfecting its constitution and its agencies to meet the extent and grandeur of its tasks'. He also encourages Christians to 'join with others in working for the good of the whole human race ... profiting by the guidance which their Christian faith provides and under the impulse of Christian love' (Pope John XXIII, 1980: para. 145).

Both Temple and John XXIII write at a very general level, avoiding detailed political conclusions (although Temple does include some in an appendix, claiming to write there as an individual rather than as an archbishop). However, they share a similar One Kingdom approach to Christian ethics. Christians are a part of society and must be concerned to promote the common good. They are not semi-detached from society with their pilgrim eyes set firmly upon the heavenly city.

The political theologian and Jesuit **David Hollenbach** and the feminist theologian **Margaret Farley** both belong to a similar Catholic natural law tradition. However, they are less bound than Temple or John XXIII by the protocols of high ecclesiastical office.

In contrast to Miranda, Hollenbach, a long-term adviser to the American Catholic Bishops on economic and political issues, is not committed to the Marxist terms that typify much liberation theology. In his 2002 book *The Common Good and Christian Ethics* he makes an extended case for the relevance of the concept of the common good for addressing certain pressing global issues, such as race, poverty and social isolation within cities:

> The growing *de facto* interdependence in both national and international life requires a stronger vision of the goods we share in common. It calls for exploration of how the well-being of individual people might be advanced by seeking goods we must share in common if we are to have them at all (Hollenbach, 2002:59–60).

Interestingly he argues that John XXIII's call for world government is too simplistic:

> The issue is more complex than this. Pursuit of the shared good under conditions of interdependence will make normative demands on nearly all people and communities. These range from intimate relationships and families, through local, national, and regional communities that are geographically defined, to historically rooted religious and cultural communities that cut across borders, to the growing number of new transnational associations that include both corporations and NGOs. The behavior of all these communities will have an impact on whether interdependence leads to common goods or common bads (Hollenbach, 2002:230–231).

It will be seen in Chapter 4 that the concept of the common good is particularly relevant to the global issue of climate change.

Farley's feminist and prophetic work on AIDS was outlined briefly in Chapter 1. However, these two short quotations from the same work indicate her inter-faith version of the One Kingdom approach to Christian ethics:

> The AIDS crisis ... presents a clear situation in which faith traditions must address their own traditional teachings about sexuality, and they must rethink the gender bias that remains deep within their teachings and practices. It would be naive to think that cultural patterns that make women vulnerable to AIDS are not influenced by world religions (and vice versa) whose presence is longstanding in their countries ...
>
> Questions must be pressed about the role of patriarchal religions in making women invisible – even though women's responsibilities are massive, and their own agency can be crucial and strong.
> If religious traditions have anything at all to say to situations like the AIDS pandemic, they must speak of God; and they must speak of human responsibilities to one another in relation to God ... The great human and religious goals of mutual respect, solidarity, fairness, compassion, come slowly (Farley, 2009:59–68).

Once again there is a mixture here of natural law and faith-based appeals.

## CASE-STUDY 1: THE MIGRATION CRISIS

Africa, Europe, Australia and the Americas today are facing a political dilemma about the current levels and social effects of mass immigration. Refugees from conflict zones and impoverished peoples seeking financial security, together and separately, challenge wealthy nations. Fears are frequently expressed about the risk both of terrorists entering countries posing as refugees and of impoverished immigrants flooding employment markets to the detriment of existing citizens.

How might Christian ethics address the current migration crisis?

By now it should be evident that Christian ethicists are unlikely to speak with a single voice. Much will depend upon which approach they adopt within the discipline.

**A natural law approach** might argue that, by nature, human beings are not just social beings. Human beings – especially those human beings whose remote ancestors left Africa to populate the world – are also by nature migrant beings. Even within Africa's remaining populations, internal migration has been widespread over time.

Mass tourism and mass pilgrimages – popular within affluent populations around the world – also provide continuing evidence of urban-dwelling humans being migrants by nature. It is not simply hunter-gathers who feel an urge to migrate. Migration of one sort or another appears to be a part of the human condition.

Some ethicists might conclude from this observation that there is a human right to migrate, provided that it does not harm other people and, therefore, there is also a duty or obligation on everyone in wealthy countries not to prevent harmless migration. The principles of fairness and freedom suggest as much.

Christian ethicists might go further at this point. The neighbour-love command of Jesus, especially when linked in Luke's Gospel to the Parable of the Good Samaritan, makes care and **hospitality to the stranger in need** a requirement for Christians:

> Just then a lawyer stood up to test Jesus. 'Teacher,' he said, 'what must I do to inherit eternal life?' He said to him, 'What is written in the law? What do you read there?' He answered, 'You shall love the Lord your God with all your heart, and with all your soul, and with all your strength, and with all your mind; and your neighbour as yourself.' And he said to him, 'You have given the right answer; do this, and you will live.' But wanting to justify himself, he asked Jesus, 'And who is my neighbour?' Jesus replied, 'A man was going down from Jerusalem to Jericho, and fell into the hands of robbers, who stripped him, beat him, and went away, leaving him half dead. Now by chance a priest was going down that road; and when he saw him, he passed by on the other side. So likewise a Levite, when he came to the place and saw him, passed by on the other side. But a Samaritan while travelling came near him; and when he saw him, he was moved with pity. He went to him and bandaged his wounds, having poured oil and wine on them. Then he put him on his own animal, brought him to an inn, and took care of him. The next day he took out two denarii, gave them to the innkeeper, and said, "Take care of him; and when I

come back, I will repay you whatever more you spend." Which of these three, do you think, was a neighbour to the man who fell into the hands of the robbers?' He said, 'The one who showed him mercy.' Jesus said to him, 'Go and do likewise' (Luke 10.25–37).

Using this parable, **Robert Heimburger**'s 2018 book *God and the Illegal Alien* argues at length for **compassion** and hospitality towards migrants, focusing upon the obligations of the United States to its Mexican workers.

**Mona Siddiqui**'s 2015 book *Hospitality and Islam* broadens this claim, arguing that all three of the Abrahamic faiths (Judaism, Christianity and Islam) have similar teaching on hospitality to strangers in need. Manifestly, refugees are strangers in need.

**Two Kingdoms approaches** might reach a similar conclusion but by a different route. They might start, instead, by appealing, say, to Galatians 3.26–29:

In Christ Jesus you are all children of God through faith. As many of you as were baptized into Christ have clothed yourselves with Christ. There is no longer Jew or Greek, there is no longer slave or free, there is no longer male and female; for all of you are one in Christ Jesus. And if you belong to Christ, then you are Abraham's offspring, heirs according to the promise.

Proponents of this approach might argue that becoming a Christian breaks down these natural (but sinful) divisions based upon ethnicity, status and gender – divisions that also affect migrants. Once baptised into Christ all are recognised as children of God. Refugees and financial immigrants who are baptised are also 'clothed with Christ' and must be treated as being one in Christ.

Heimburger adds a further point here. In major Western cities, such as New York or London, immigrants now play a major role in many local congregations. In this context, immigration, far from being 'a problem' for churches, has actually boosted their otherwise declining membership.

Expressed in this way there are **two major differences** between these two approaches – the status of what is considered to be 'natural' and the relevance of their conclusions to non-Christians.

Aquinas recognises frankly that perceptions of what is natural can be distorted by bad customs and sin. Nevertheless, he is convinced that reason can sift out these distortions and allow us to reach firm conclusions about what really is 'natural'.

However, modified natural law exponents today tend to be more cautious. They point out that even Aquinas was wrong, for example, about men being by nature more rational than women. As a result, modified natural law exponents typically treat 'nature' as an indicator but not as a rule-maker for ethical judgments. So, for them, the observation that human beings are prone to migration would not necessarily mean that they have a right to migrate.

The Two Kingdoms approach usually goes further than this, maintaining that human nature is so distorted by sin that it is not even an indicator for reliable ethical judgments. Faith in Christ is the only ethical authority for them.

But this raises the other issue, namely the relevance of Christian decisions about ethics for non-Christians. A natural law approach starts from a position that can – in theory *but not always in practice* – be shared by Christians and non-Christians alike, before moving to more demanding precepts that are distinctively Christian. A Two Kingdoms approach, in its strictest form, insists that *people need to come to faith in Christ* before they are able to make reliable ethical judgments.

The italics in this paragraph highlight difficulties facing each approach. It may also help to explain why neither Aquinas nor Luther (let alone Augustine) is fully consistent on ethical issues. To put this bluntly, Aquinas is not always rational when he thinks he is being rational and Luther is not always biblical when he thinks he is being biblical.

It is at this point that some recent contextual approaches to Christian ethics may be more helpful. In particular, differing perspectives from liberation theology, post-colonial theology, and feminist and womanist theology may give greater nuance.

A central feature of **liberation theology** is its 'bias to the poor'. Faced with the plight of Mexican workers in the United States, many of whom, in legal terms, are illegal aliens, a liberation theologian would be likely to champion their cause and not that of their much-wealthier critics. Wealthy Americans employ Mexican workers because they provide cheap and ready labour. Similarly, wealthy British people buy goods manufactured by poorly paid workers in Asia because they are cheap and disposable. For the liberation theologian this is exploitation.

**Post-colonial theology** adds an extra dimension to this critique. The British Empire, and other similar empires, exploited poorer countries, most shockingly through the slave trade, in past centuries. Britain continues to benefit from the wealth created by that exploitation and has a duty to rebalance it, not least in accepting immigrants from countries that it previously exploited. Accepting these immigrants is not a matter of charity but an obligation for restitution.

**Feminist and womanist theology** adds a sharper focus upon women and children. Margaret Farley's approach to Christian ethics, based upon compassionate respect, might well observe that women of colour and children refugees are frequently treated poorly. They do not always receive adequate health care and are sometimes held in crowded and badly maintained conditions while they await settlement.

These contextual approaches refocus the ethical discussion of a particular issue. Instead of offering universal 'solutions', they are self-consciously biased towards the disadvantaged – the poor, the exploited and those who suffer from discrimination – just as Jesus, in Luke's Gospel especially, was.

Does this mean that Christian ethicists are bound to support human migration wherever it occurs? Even in the tentative suggestion above, that human beings may have a right to migrate, the words 'provided that it does not harm other people' were added.

Mass migration that is beyond the capacity of a receiving country to cope with may constitute such a harm. If the account already given of Aquinas's teaching is followed, it is the duty of rulers to protect all that they govern, ensuring the health of the inhabitants, their security from being attacked, and that they have sufficient physical sustenance. Mass migration that puts this duty at risk might, therefore, be opposed.

The risk of terrorists entering countries posing as refugees is another, potentially greater, harm. This issue is also highly pertinent to faith-based forms of ethics. As noted in the further reading in the Introduction, there is a substantial literature now on religiously inspired violence. Although there is debate on the extent and exact causes of this violence across different religions, it is clear that the destruction of the Twin Towers in New York in the 9/11 attack, and similar acts of violence since then, have had a religiously inspired component.

One of the important points that this raises for Christian ethics is about how violent texts within the Bible are to be understood (Chapter 8 will look at these texts in more detail). The annihilation texts (*herem* in Hebrew, meaning 'ban') within Deuteronomy are particularly offensive when taken literally:

> When the Lord your God brings you into the land that you are about to enter and occupy, and he clears away many nations before you— the Hittites, the Girgashites, the Amorites, the Canaanites, the Perizzites, the Hivites, and the Jebusites, seven nations mightier and more numerous than you— and when the Lord your God gives them over to you and you defeat them, then you must utterly destroy them. Make no covenant with them and show them no mercy ... You shall devour all the peoples that the Lord your God is giving over to you, showing them no pity (7.1–2 & 16).

> But as for the towns of these peoples that the Lord your God is giving you as an inheritance, you must not let anything that breathes remain alive. You shall annihilate them (20.16–17).

As a young man Augustine was deeply shocked by such texts, particularly if they are combined with the statement attributed to Jesus in Matthew: 'Do not think that I have come to bring peace to the earth; I have not come to bring peace, but a sword' (10.34). They may well have contributed to his initial reluctance to accept the Christian faith.

Are these texts really very different from, say, the following command in the Qur'an: 'Whenever you encounter the idolaters, kill them, seize them, besiege them, wait for them at every lookout post' (Sura 9.5)?

This question raises a crucial issue for Chapter 3, namely whether or not Christian ethics can accept that some acts of violence (especially wars) are justified.

## FURTHER READING

All the quotations of the following authors in this chapter can be found in greater detail in Section 2 of my *A Textbook of Christian Ethics*:

Aquinas, Thomas (1948), De Regimine Principum, XII–XIV (On Princely Government, from A.P. D'Entrèves [ed], *Aquinas: Selected Political Writings*, Oxford: Blackwell, trans. J.G. Dawson, pp. 67–77).

Augustine (1972), in David Knowles (ed), *The City of God* XIX. 14–17 (London: Pelican Classics, trans. Henry Bettenson, pp. 872–879).

Barrera, Albino (2011), *Market Complicity and Christian Ethics* (New York and Cambridge: Cambridge University Press). This is a demanding, advanced level book and part of the New Studies in Christian Ethics series.

Hauerwas, Stanley (1983) [1984], *The Peaceable Kingdom* (Notre Dame, IN: University of Notre Dame Press, and London: SCM Press).

Lovin, Robin W. (2008), *Christian Realism and the New Realities* (New York and Cambridge: Cambridge University Press). This book is excellent, but it is at an advanced level.

Luther, Martin (1966), Trade and Usury in *Luther's Works* (Vol. 45, Philadelphia: Fortress Press, trans. Charles M. Jacobs and Rev.Walther I. Brandt, pp. 245–246, 247–254 & 255–260).

Siddiqui, Mona (2012), *The Good Muslim* (Cambridge: Cambridge University Press).

Siddiqui, Mona (2014), *Christians, Muslims and Jesus* (New Haven, CT, and London: Yale University Press).

## REFERENCES

Barrera, Albino (2005), *Economic Compulsion and Christian Ethics* (New York and Cambridge: Cambridge University Press). This is a demanding, advanced level book and part of the New Studies in Christian Ethics series.

Barth, Karl (1929), *The Epistle to the Romans* (Oxford: Oxford University Press, on Rom. 13.21 & 14.1). Fairly accessible.

Berdyaev, Nicolas (1935), *Freedom and the Spirit* (London: Geoffrey Bles Centenary Press, pp. x–xiv and xvi–xviii). Less accessible.

Bowler, Kate (2013), *Blessed: A History of the American Prosperity Gospel* (Oxford: Oxford University Press). Fairly accessible.

Calvin, John. *Commentary on the Epistle to the Romans* (trans. John Owen) and *Commentary on Daniel* (trans. Thomas Meyers). Available online at: https://www.ccel.org/ccel/calvin/commentaries.i.html (accessed 1/7/19).

Farley, Margaret A. (2009), Essay 1 in Gillian Patterson (ed), *HIV Prevention: A Global Conversation* (Geneva: Ecumenical Advocacy Alliance, pp. 59–68). See also a mention of her in the References at the end of Chapter 1. Accessible.

Hauerwas, Stanley (1974), *Vision and Virtue* (Notre Dame, IN: Fides).

Hauerwas, Stanley & Willimon, William (1989), *Resident Aliens: Life in the Christian Colony* (Nashville, TN: Abingdon). This is very accessible, albeit highly polemical. Hauerwas is probably the most widely read Christian ethicist today, helped by the fact that he tends to avoid jargon and adopts forceful positions.

Heimburger, Robert W. (2018), *God and the Illegal Alien: Unites States Immigration Law and a Theology of Politics* (Cambridge: Cambridge University Press). Advanced level.

Hollenbach, David, S.J. (2002), *The Common Good and Christian Ethics* (New York and Cambridge: Cambridge University Press, pp. 56–60 & 229–231). This fairly advanced-level book is part of the New Studies in Christian Ethics series.

Lovin, Robin W. (1995), *Reinhold Niebuhr and Christian Realism* (New York and Cambridge: Cambridge University Press). This book is excellent, but it is at an advanced level.

Miranda, José Porfirio (1977), *Marx and the Bible* (London: SCM Press, and New York: Orbis Books, trans. John Eagleson, pp. 14–22). Advanced level.

Niebuhr, Reinhold (1960), *Moral Man and Immoral Society* (New York: Scribner, reissue, pp. 257–259 & 268–275). Fairly accessible.

Pope John XXIII (1980), *Pacem in Terris* (London: Catholic Truth Society, reissue, trans. HenryWaterhouseS.J., paras. 80–96, 130–146 & 161–171) and available online at: http://www.vatican.va/content/john-xxiii/en/encyclicals/documents/hf_j-xxiii_enc_11041963_pacem.html

Siddiqui, Mona (2015), *Hospitality and Islam: Welcoming in God's Name* (New Haven, CT, and London: Yale University Press). Advanced level.

Temple, William (1976), *Christianity and Social Order* (London: Shepheard-Walwyn & SPCK, reissue, pp. 58–59, 60–62, 67–68, 69–71, 72–74, 75 & 77). Very accessible.

Quotations from the Qur'an come from M.A.S Abdel Haleem's translation (Oxford: Oxford World's Classics, 2008).

# 3

# WAR AND PEACE

Chapter 2 ended with a question, namely whether or not Christian ethicists can accept that some wars are justified. Once Christianity was adopted as the official religion of the Roman Empire in the 4th century this question could hardly be avoided. If empires are to survive they need to be protected from potential usurpers, and it is difficult to do that without an army.

It is likely that some of the earliest Christians were soldiers. Both Matthew and Luke tell a similar story of a Roman centurion who appeals to Jesus to heal his sick servant, or slave. In both forms of this story Jesus expresses strong admiration for the centurion's faith. As already noted, Matthew also attributes the following saying to Jesus: 'Do not think that I have come to bring peace to the earth; I have not come to bring peace, but a sword' (10.34). In addition, Luke even ascribes the following unusually military parable to Jesus:

> What king, going out to wage war against another king, will not sit down first and consider whether he is able with ten thousand to oppose the one who comes against him with twenty thousand? If he cannot, then, while the other is still far away, he sends a delegation and asks for the terms of peace (14.31–32).

And Paul, at times, uses swords and armour as metaphors for depicting Christian faith.

However, if used as evidence of Jesus accepting warfare, none of these examples is very convincing. More obviously they are all metaphors for discipleship, as the next verse in Luke clearly shows:

'So therefore, none of you can become my disciple if you do not give up all your possessions' (14.33).

In addition, it seems likely that, even if some of the earliest Christians were soldiers, they were soldiers first who subsequently became Christians. An inescapable feature of Roman military service before the 4th century was an obligation to make sacrifices and/or oaths to Roman gods – an obligation that is nothing but idolatry for the theologian Tertullian (c.160–220).

Tertullian also insists that, despite the story of the centurion's faith, Jesus's subsequent disarming of Peter at Gethsemane (a story told in all four Gospels but only identified with Peter in John 18.10–11) takes away the sword from all soldiers. Tertullian takes an absolutist stance against any form of homicide – military, civil or even medical. But, of course, Tertullian has no obligation to defend the army of a non-Christian Roman Empire.

In contrast, now that the Roman Empire has adopted Christianity, Augustine, writing two centuries later, does feel such an obligation.

## AUGUSTINE ON JUSTIFIED HOMICIDE

For nine years, from the age of 19, **Augustine** (c. 354–430) was, as noted earlier, a follower of Manichaeism – a dualistic and sectarian form of faith. Following his baptism and then ordination as a Catholic Christian, and shortly before becoming Bishop of Hippo, he wrote his *Reply to Faustus the Manichaean* in about 397, the same time that he wrote his *Confessions*.

By this stage Augustine has been deeply impressed by the Catholic Bishop of Milan, Ambrose, and seriously disillusioned by meeting the Manichaean Bishop, Faustus. Frankly, he finds Ambrose to be wise and cultured, but Faustus to be quite the reverse. He is also attracted by Ambrose's distinction between just and unjust forms of warfare, but repelled by Faustus's sectarian rejection of warfare.

Augustine acknowledges at the outset that the Patriarch Moses once killed an Egyptian (Exodus 2.12). Was this killing of an oppressor justified? He judges that it was not, because, in terms of 'the eternal law, it was wrong for one who had no legal authority to kill'. So, for Augustine, this act of homicide was wrong because it was committed without the authority either of God or of a legal authority.

Like Tertullian, Augustine argues that Peter's action in Gethsemane was also unjustified, albeit for a very different reason:

> It was the same with Peter, when he took his sword out of its sheath to defend the Lord, and cut off the right ear of an assailant, when the Lord rebuked him with something like a threat, saying, 'Put up your sword into its sheath; for he that takes the sword shall perish by the sword.' To take the sword is to use weapons against a person's life, without the sanction of the constituted authority. The Lord, indeed, had told the disciples to carry a sword; but he did not tell them to use it.

But what of the plagues inflicted later through Moses that killed many Egyptians ahead of the exodus of Israelites from Egypt? Were these acts of violence and homicide justified? Here Augustine argues that they were indeed justified since they were done 'by the command of God': 'God's commands are to be submissively received, not to be argued against.' Indeed, 'Moses could not lawfully have done otherwise than God told him, leaving to God the reason of the command, while the servant's duty is to obey'.

Augustine gives another example at this point, using the Genesis story of Abraham's thwarted attempt to sacrifice his son Isaac to God: 'For Abraham to sacrifice his son of his own accord is shocking madness. His doing so at the command of God proves him faithful and submissive.'

Augustine is highly critical of Faustus's moral scruples about Old Testament violence (scruples which he probably shared in his own Manichaean youth). He argues bluntly:

> The account of the wars of Moses will not excite surprise or abhorrence, for in wars carried on by divine command, he showed not ferocity but obedience; and God, in giving the command, acted not in cruelty, but in righteous retribution, giving to all what they deserved, and warning those who needed warning. What is the evil in war? Is it the death of some who will soon die in any case, that others may live in peaceful subjection? This is mere cowardly dislike, not any religious feeling.

In short, both genocide and child sacrifice are justified if undertaken in response to God's command. This is a mightily strong version of **command ethics**.

The highly intelligent Augustine is trying to reconcile a number of competing commitments that still trouble many Christians today.

There is a commitment to civil authority and social order. It has already been seen that Luther, Calvin, Barth and Bonhoeffer all share this commitment (albeit with differences between them on whether or not to respect tyrants). All of them, including Augustine, refer explicitly to Romans 13.1: 'Let every person be subject to the governing authorities.'

There is a commitment to neighbour-love and peace, as seen already in Chapter 2. Augustine's commitment here is sometimes summarised by the aphorism 'love and do what you will', based upon his so-called love sermon on 1 John 4.4–12. However, it should be noted that this sermon also contains the advice: 'Do not imagine that you love your servant when you refrain from beating him.'

There is a commitment to the Bible, including sections on violence that Augustine once found deeply problematic. He regards Faustus as being highly selective in his use of the Bible (cherry-picking again).

Yet there are obvious weaknesses in each of these commitments. Beating servants, let alone having bonded slaves, while perhaps acceptable to 4th century Roman householders is obviously not in the 21st century. At this point Augustine appears thoroughly anachronistic. His version of 'tough-love' owes more to the prevailing Roman culture than to his Christian faith.

In addition, Augustine's commitment to authority, divine or human, is remarkably unconditional. Religious fanatics who commit acts of terror in the 21st century typically invoke the authority of God to justify their actions. 'God is great' has become the slogan of many suicide-bombers. Some secularists argue that this provides primary evidence that all religious belief is dangerous and should be eliminated from society. Manifestly religiously inspired terrorism polarises attitudes towards authority.

In contrast, people of faith might argue that religiously inspired terrorists have seriously misinterpreted divine authority. These terrorists have read violent texts in the Qur'an or in the Bible out of context and jumped to the conclusion that they remain God's commands for the world today. Unlike Augustine, the medieval Jewish philosopher Maimonides argued that such a jump from Deuteronomy to his day was unjustified.

Another problem with Augustine's interpretation of the Old Testament is that it is not always consistent. This will become apparent in Chapter 5 when Augustine discusses the Old Testament's celebrated suicide-bomber, Samson. It was Samson who deliberately pulled down the pillars of a house, in the process killing himself and thousands of Philistine men and women (Judges 16.30). Unfortunately for Augustine's theory of justified homicide, Judges makes no mention of God commanding Samson to act in this way. So Augustine argues that the Spirit 'secretly ordered him to do so' – a classic argument from silence.

Augustine's commitment to civil authority is also remarkably unconditional. The standard excuse of those being tried for war crimes in the modern world is that they were only acting 'on authority'. The political leaders were to blame not the military. However, that excuse is precisely what was disallowed at the Nürnberg Trials after the Second Word War. Blind military obedience to an unjust civil authority was judged to be culpable, not praiseworthy.

**Thomas Aquinas** does quote from Augustine here, but he also adds to his analysis and, in the process, helps to develop a somewhat more adequate Just War theory.

## AQUINAS ON JUST WAR AND THE CLERGY

*Summa Theologica* asks four questions regarding warfare:

- Is it always a sin to wage war?
- May clergy and bishops engage in war?
- May belligerents use subterfuge?
- May war be waged on feast days?

It is the first question that is most relevant here. However, Aquinas does have some telling points to make about why clergy and bishops should be exempt from military service.

He is aware at the outset that some people believe warfare is always sinful – citing Matthew's Sermon on the Mount (5.39) and his unique addition to Jesus's warning at Gethsemane that 'all who take the sword will perish by the sword' (26.52). Aquinas also tests the idea that, since peace is a virtue, war as the opposite of peace is not virtuous but sinful.

On the other hand, he argues, Jesus's response to the centurion demonstrates that he 'did not forbid a military career'.

Aquinas then sets out three criteria needed for any war to be just.

- The first is 'the authority of the sovereign on whose command war is engaged'. Here he follows Augustine's main point that private individuals cannot properly declare war or summon people to fight a war. Only those in authority can do so.
- The second is that 'a just cause is required, namely that those who are attacked are attacked because they deserve it on account of some wrong they have done'.
- The third is that 'the right intention of those waging war is required, that is, they must intend to promote the good and avoid evil'.

He then clarifies this, adding that the authority of God can also justify someone spilling human blood, as can someone acting 'for the common good or even for the good of his opponents'. He also adds that 'those who wage a just war intend peace'.

Why does Aquinas believe that clergy and bishops should not engage in war? Here he contrasts sharply with both Tertullian and Augustine. As just seen, for Tertullian the disarming of Peter at Gethsemane takes away the sword from all soldiers. For Augustine, however, it shows that violence 'without the sanction of the constituted authority' is sinful. But for Aquinas this is simply a command addressed to (Pope) Peter:

> The words, 'Put your sword back in its scabbard' were directed to Peter as representing all bishops and clerics. Consequently, they may not fight.

He gives two additional reasons. The first is that the upsetting conditions of war 'prevent the mind from contemplating divine things'. The second is that the sacred office of those ordained 'is not to kill or to shed blood, but rather to be ready to shed their own blood for Christ, to do in deed what they portray at the altar'.

## STRENGTHS

Aquinas adds significantly to Augustine. He sets out the three criteria for any war to be just as if they were all equally present in Augustine's position on war. In reality Augustine overwhelmingly emphasises legitimate authority (human or divine) as *the* criterion allowing him to distinguish between justified and unjustified homicide. Aquinas goes considerably beyond this.

In particular, Aquinas gives all three criteria – legitimate authority, just cause, and right intention – equal space. By adding 'acting for the common good' and 'intending peace' he goes further still. There are the makings here of the fuller Just War criteria that would be expected today in discussions of military ethics.

On the question of whether clergy should engage in war, Aquinas again anticipates some elements of modern military ethics. There is still a strong reluctance today to see military chaplains actively involved in killing within warfare or even carrying arms. Their role is generally seen to be that of supporting active service personnel, both pastorally and liturgically, but not in purely military terms. Military chaplains, like military medical doctors, have a difficult dual role – emphatically being professional clergy or doctors while being paid by military authorities.

Aquinas recognises parts of this dual role. Clergy cannot engage in war or even (as he argues later) take an active part in jousting since it simulates war. Yet they can support those who fight in properly authorised wars. Indeed, through his setting out of Just War criteria, that is exactly what he is doing himself.

## WEAKNESSES

Yet Aquinas does little to resolve the problems of authority (human or divine) that face Augustine's notion of legitimate authority. Critics have pointed out that Aquinas's Italy had a plethora of 'princes' and that members of his own family served rival princes. So, obeying 'the authority of the sovereign on whose command war is engaged' was, in practice, no straightforward matter – either for his family or, three centuries later, for Luther. Aquinas simply glosses over this problem.

It will also be seen in a moment that there are distinctions in modern Just War theory that Aquinas never envisaged. Today it is usually considered to be good practice to distinguish between just causes for going to war, just practices within war, and just policies after war. Also, with hindsight, some of Aquinas's criteria are undeveloped and other modern criteria are simply missing. For example, there is the crucial criterion developed in later centuries that before going to war all peaceful means of avoiding war must be exhausted.

Of course, it would be unreasonable to expect Aquinas to anticipate everything – especially today, when military weapons have become so destructive. In retrospect, he lived in quite a peaceful time in Europe and experienced nothing to compare with the horrors of the First World War. As a result, his discussion of war is never very extensive and appears by modern standards to be highly formulaic. Both Augustine and Luther lived in much more dangerous times and their expressions of distress about the perils of warfare are much stronger than anything articulated by Aquinas.

Aquinas's interpretation of the story of the disarming of Peter at Gethsemane also raises huge problems that continue today. When comparing Tertullian, Augustine and Aquinas on this issue it is difficult not to reach the conclusion that their different social contexts have radically affected their divergent interpretations. Radical pacifism for Tertullian, legitimate authority for homicide for Augustine, and clerical exemption from war for Aquinas are *extraordinarily* different interpretations.

Does that matter for Christian ethics? Well, yes, it does. It will be seen in Chapter 5 that Christian ethicists have diverged radically from each other over the last few decades on how to interpret biblical texts on sexuality. Radical divisions over sexuality have threated schisms within a number of Christian denominations and, so far, appear to be intractable.

Aquinas himself appears oblivious to the radically different ways that the story of the disarming of Peter at Gethsemane had been interpreted in the 1,000 years that separate him from Tertullian. A full historical account of biblical interpretation poses a very serious and ongoing problem for Christian ethics.

And **Martin Luther**, when writing on war, adds to the problem.

## LUTHER ON SOLDIERS AND OBEDIENCE

Luther wrote *Whether Soldiers, too, Can be Saved* in 1526. He was still smarting from the fierce reaction to his notorious treatise, written the previous year, *Against the Robbing and Murderous Hordes of Peasants*. In the latter he urged rulers to put down a widespread popular insurrection and to kill the rebels (some of whom had actually expected his support):

> For rebellion is not just simple murder; it is like a great fire, which attacks and devastates a whole land. Therefore let everyone who can, smite, slay, and stab, secretly or openly, remembering that nothing can be more poisonous, hurtful, or devilish than a rebel. It is just as when one must kill a mad dog.

His tone in *Whether Soldiers, too, Can be Saved* is considerably less harsh, but he still insists, with a considerable degree of anger, that rebellion is wrong and that rebels should submit – and be forced to submit – to the authority of (good or bad) rulers.

Luther recognises frankly that war is 'a great plague' and seems contrary to 'works of love'. However, he likens a soldier's office to that of a surgeon who amputates diseased parts of a living body. Such a surgeon 'appears to be cruel and merciless' but in reality is doing 'good and Christian work':

> In the same way, when I think of a soldier fulfilling his office by punishing the wicked, killing the wicked, and creating so much misery, it seems an un-Christian work completely contrary to Christian love. But when I think of how it protects the good and keeps and preserves wife and child, house and farm, property, and honour and peace, then I see how precious and godly this work is.

He also recognises that some soldiers abuse their office and 'kill people needlessly simply because they want to'. But he reminds his readers that 'in the end God's justice finds them and strikes, as happened to the peasants in the revolt'. Such abuse should not be used as an argument against the military and in favour of popular revolt: 'If the waging of war and the military profession were in themselves wrong and displeasing to God, we should have to condemn Abraham, Moses, Joshua, David, and all the rest of the holy fathers, kings, and princes, who served God as soldiers and are highly praised in Scripture because of this service.'

Luther is emphatic that the 'office of the sword is in itself right and is a divine and useful ordinance, which God does not want us to despise, but to fear, honour, and obey, under penalty of punishments as St Paul says in Romans 13'.

But what if a ruler is mad? Should such a ruler be obeyed? Here Luther makes a distinction between 'mad' and 'tyrant'. If mad, then the ruler, lacking reason, should be deposed. However, if a tyrant (who may in fact do greater harm than one who is mad) then not so, because 'if it is considered right to murder or depose tyrants, the practice spreads and it becomes a commonplace thing arbitrarily to call men tyrants who are not tyrants, and even to kill them if the mob takes a notion to do so'.

Luther does not believe in encouraging 'the mob'. For him the mob 'goes mad too quickly'. Vengeance should be left to God (Romans 12.19), not to the mob. God has all sorts of ways of punishing tyrants.

He realises at this point that some will claim he is 'flattering the princes'. His response is to point out, accurately, that 'they will not be very happy to receive this flattery'. In his view, despite his jaundiced opinion about some princes/rulers, they are to be obeyed.

But what if one of these rulers is wrong in going to war? Here Luther responds, perhaps surprisingly, to the questioner: 'you should neither fight nor serve, for you cannot have a good conscience before God.' And people who decide to take this path should simply accept the personal consequences of their decision.

Equally surprising is his response to the question of whether a soldier can serve for, and be paid by, different rulers:

> A craftsman may sell his skill to anyone who will have it, and thus serve the one to whom he sells it, so long as this is not against his ruler and his community. In the same way a soldier has his skill in fighting from God and can use it in the service of whoever desires to have it, exactly as though his skill were an art or trade, and he can take pay for it as he would for his work.

However, Luther does warn such soldiers (in effect mercenaries), just as he was seen in Chapter 2 to warn merchants that 'greed is wrong'. Providing that people are not greedy, they can sell their marketable skills – military or non-military.

## STRENGTHS

Luther gives robust answers to difficult questions. He is also passionate and probably more than a bit hurt by criticism from both rebels and rulers. These criticisms polarised many of the Reformers, with some joining the rebels, some siding with Luther, and others adopting a position of radical pacifism and disengagement from society at large. These were deeply troubling times.

Despite his bombastic rhetoric, Luther shows that he is well aware of the perils of what he regards as legitimate warfare. However, for him, these perils are offset by the disastrous effects of popular rebellion. Soldiers are, in the end, peacekeepers. Some may abuse their office, but overall their office is essential for peace.

In addition, despite his heavy emphasis upon civil obedience, Luther does allow for individual conscience and for the removal of rulers who are simply mad. So there is nuance to his otherwise dogmatic position.

## WEAKNESSES

Nevertheless there are also striking weaknesses in this treatise.

Compared with Aquinas, a very obvious weakness is Luther's lack of criteria for Just War or for just rule. If warfare, or the threat of warfare, is essential for maintaining a peaceful society (as most Just War exponents claim), are there ethical limits to such warfare? In a world that now has the capacity for devastating nuclear warfare, this question is more pertinent than ever. But Luther leaves readers fairly clueless about how to respond.

His defence of mercenaries is also very unusual within Christian ethics. Is the skill of being able to kill people, without believing that one is doing this to defend one's own country, really in accordance with Christian ethics? Few Christian ethicists today would respond with a 'yes' to that question.

Luther, like Augustine, is a relentless polemicist. He argues for a position through his attacks on opponents. This means that his (and Augustine's) position on particular issues can change and result in self-contradiction, depending upon which opponents he is attacking. Comparing *Whether Soldiers, too, Can be Saved* with *Against the Robbing and Murderous Hordes of Peasants*, this much becomes very clear. In contrast to Aquinas, consistency is not Luther's strong suit.

His attempt to distinguish between mad rulers and tyrants illustrates this lack of consistency, especially when he also allows for individual conscience. For example, by joining the unsuccessful bomb plot to assassinate Hitler, did the Lutheran Dietrich Bonhoeffer follow Luther's teaching or not?

We can only speculate since Bonhoeffer, in prison for this act and then executed, was in no position to explain. Yet, given Luther's lack of clarity and consistency, any of the following might be possible:

- Bonhoeffer decided that Hitler, at this late stage in the Second World War, was actually mad and should, therefore, be halted.
- Bonhoeffer concluded that his individual conscience overrode his duty of obedience to Hitler as his ruler.
- Bonhoeffer realised that, by returning to Germany to oppose Hitler, he never did regard Hitler as his (legitimate) ruler.
- Bonhoeffer judged that Luther was wrong about tyrants. They should be destroyed when they are devastating the world.

Trying to follow Luther's highly influential teaching is not always easy.

## CATHOLIC JUST WAR TEACHING TODAY

The Dominican **Eberhard Welty**'s 1963 textbook, *A Handbook of Christian Social Ethics*, provides a modern example of the way that Aquinas's criteria have been developed in a nuclear age.

By the time that Welty writes, it is widely accepted that wars of pure aggression are unjustified. This position expands Aquinas's just-cause criterion, namely that an existing wrong is being addressed in a Just War. Welty warns that 'the most senseless local conflict can easily develop into a world war'.

Yet he admits frankly that it is difficult to state exactly which wars are to be considered to be wars of aggression. The Korean War had already raised this very issue in the 1950s. The issue also became a point of fierce contention later in the wars within the Middle East in the final years of the 20th century. Welty recognises that 'wars of aggression are not confined to unjust, wilful attacks, for they may have just causes, such as the infringement or the denial of essential rights'.

So how do we decide whether a particular war is a war of aggression? Welty's answer (similar to that of Pope John XXIII in Chapter 2) is that we must let an 'international tribunal' make the decision.

Welty offers three criteria for a defensive war to be considered lawful:

- There must be an unjust, actual attack that cannot otherwise be met.
- The aggressor must not be harmed more than is necessary.
- The defence must have a prospect of success, and no higher goods must be jeopardised than those which have to be defended.

It is the third criterion that particularly post-dates Aquinas. Arguably it is implicit in the unusually military parable mentioned earlier (Luke 14.31–32). Some have claimed that this parable has more to do with prudence than ethics. It would, after all, be foolish for people to fight wars that they knew they would lose (although sadly some people do just that). Others argue, to the contrary, that fighting such a war is unethical because it results in pointless killing.

For Welty, wars of liberation are particularly open to this dilemma and can only be justified if they have a 'solid probability' of success:

> Since the good and ill of all humanity is at stake, all States and groups of States are obliged to participate if necessary, and the organised community of nations has undoubtedly the right to impose this obligation. Real interdependence among the nations should form the

most effective defence and be most likely to avert such a war of liberation. Power that tends to disrupt can only be kept in check by the
threat and the readiness for defence of a bigger power (Welty,
1963:420–421).

Welty is also very conscious that modern nuclear warfare has
become so destructive of civilian populations, and 'such a menace to
world peace', that it can only be justified if it is wholly defensive.
He thinks that it is possible to distinguish ethically between holding
nuclear weapons as deterrents and using them uncontrollably in a
war. However, after the Cuban missile crisis in the previous year this
was already a debatable distinction.

Twenty years after Welty the **United States Catholic Bishops'**
1983 pastoral letter, *The Challenge of Peace*, avoids this distinction
and, instead, concludes emphatically that 'the nuclear age is an era of
moral as well as physical danger':

> In simple terms, we are saying that good ends (defending one's coun-
> try, protecting freedom, etc.) cannot justify immoral means (the use of
> weapons which kill indiscriminately and threaten whole societies). We
> fear that our world and nation are headed in the wrong direction. More
> weapons with greater destructive potential are produced every day.
> More and more nations are seeking to become nuclear powers. In our
> quest for more and more security, we fear we are actually becoming
> less and less secure (US Catholic Bishops, 1983: para. 332).

Remarkably the bishops break away from the traditional Catholic
teaching that sees, following Aquinas, Just War as the only legitimate position on war. Instead, they treat Just War *and* pacifist
traditions as both contributing 'to the full moral vision we need in
pursuit of a human peace':

> We believe the two perspectives support and complement one
> another, each preserving the other from distortion. Finally, in an age
> of technological warfare, analysis from the viewpoint of non-violence
> and analysis from the viewpoint of the just-war teaching often con-
> verge and agree in their opposition to methods of warfare which are
> in fact indistinguishable from total warfare (US Catholic Bishops,
> 1983: para. 121).

In short, for them, Just War and pacifist perspectives 'share a common presumption against the use of force as a means of settling disputes'. The nuclear era makes this presumption imperative.

Specifically, within their understanding of the Just War perspective, the bishops distinguish carefully between just causes for going to war and just practices within war.

**Just causes for going to war** they assess, as others have done, in terms of seven criteria: just cause; competent authority; comparative justice; right intention; last resort; probability of success; and proportionality. They find 'competent authority' and 'last resort' especially difficult today in democratic countries, regretting that the United Nations Organisation is still (20 years on from John XXIII) relatively powerless.

**Just practices within war** they consider simply in terms of proportionality (again) and discrimination. Proportionality in both contexts causes them huge problems in a nuclear age. They remind readers that even in the non-nuclear Vietnam War they reached the conclusion that 'the conflict had reached such a level of devastation to the adversary and damage to our own society that continuing it could not be justified'. Nuclear weapons, in addition, face massive problems of discrimination, especially given their potential for massive collateral damage on non-military populations.

In the 1980s it was not as usual, as it is today, to consider **just policies after war** as a distinct third category. Nevertheless, the bishops' promotion of non-violent action does partially address this important area.

Responding to the Catholic bishops' pastoral letter and to the United States Methodist Bishops' 1986 report, *In Defence of Creation: The Nuclear Crisis and a Just Peace*, the Catholic feminist **Lisa Sowle Cahill**'s 1994 book, *Love Your Enemies: Discipleship, Pacifism, and Just War Theory*, concludes that the Methodists make 'a much more urgent stand against war than Roman Catholicism'. She sees this particularly in the Methodists' stated commitment:

> We believe war is incompatible with the teaching and example of Christ. We therefore reject war as an instrument of national foreign policy and insist that the first moral duty of all nations is to resolve by peaceful means every dispute that arises between or among them (US Methodist Bishops, 1986: para. 40).

As a Roman Catholic she sees her own position as closer to that of the Methodist than the Catholic bishops – biased as it is in favour of pacifism, albeit without totally rejecting Just War criteria. She concludes:

> Both biblically and historically, pacifism is grounded in and experienced as consistent with a committed communal practice of forgiveness, forbearance, and fellowship. The stronger tie of the pacifist expression to recognizably Christian discipleship communities makes an obvious statement in its favour contrasted to just war thinking (Cahill, 1994:244).

How does this Catholic assessment match up to the work of Methodist ethicists in this area?

## METHODIST POSITIONS ON JUST WAR AND PACIFISM TODAY

Actually, even wider tensions on the legitimacy of war, nuclear deterrence and pacifism can be found within the contrasting ethical conclusions of Methodist theologians today.

The American Methodist **Paul Ramsey** (1913–1988) pioneered a non-Catholic use of Just War theory in his seminal 1961 book, *War and the Christian Conscience: How Shall Modern War Be Conducted Justly?* For him the Just War categories help to make ethical discussion of war more robust within Reformed Christian ethics.

Ramsey's style of writing tended to be polemical. For example, he was unusual in the 1960s for claiming that the (increasingly unpopular) American role in the Vietnam War was actually just.

Equally polemical was his strong defence of nuclear deterrence and his critique of what some theologians at the time termed 'nuclear pacifism'. His 1967 book, *Who Speaks for the Church? A Critique of the 1966 Geneva Conference on Church and Society*, articulates this pugnaciously. He argues that the anti-nuclear bias within the World Council of Churches at Geneva in the 1960s was deeply misguided:

> The *actuality* of deterrence depends upon a credible belief, mutually shared, that one might use a nuclear weapon. If the government of one of the great powers were persuaded by the churches never to be

> willing to use any nuclear weapon under any circumstances, and this were known, there would instantly be no deterrence and therefore no practical problem of finding a way out. Likewise, the *morality* of deterrence depends upon it not being wholly immoral for a government ever to use an atomic weapon under any circumstances. If those who use any nuclears in any way in any war will have God against them, God is against the possession of all these weapons right now for deterrence (Ramsey, 1967:114).

Ramsey is highly sceptical of 'ecclesiastical pronouncements' that become 'too specific' on political issues. He believes, instead, that 'Protestant Christians, whose consciences are not bound by either pope or church councils, ought to be engaged constantly in going to the theoretical roots in the examination and re-examination of any and all ecclesiastical pronouncements, instead of using these as legal instruments for keeping in repair some supposed consensus on particular policies' (1967:119).

In short, Christian ethicists lacking political expertise should not pontificate on detailed political decision-making.

A generation later the American Methodist **Stanley Hauerwas** can hardly be more different. He is not just a nuclear pacifist, he is a thoroughgoing pacifist, as his 1983 book *The Peaceable Kingdom* and 1985 book *Against the Nations* make clear.

In an important 1985 essay, 'Pacifism: Some Philosophical Considerations', Hauerwas sets out his version of pacifism in opposition to a Just War position:

> The problem with the just-war rationale for violence is that it so seldom places a limit on the use of violence. The just warrior assumes that violence can only be used as a last resort, but the very meaning of 'last resort' becomes elastic exactly because it is assumed that if things become rough we can resort to the gun we keep handy for just such emergencies. As a result we fail to become the kind of people whose very commitment to non-violence makes it possible for us to live non-violently (Hauerwas, 1985:101–102).

In contrast to Ramsey, Hauerwas insists that Christians are, or should be, people with a radical commitment to non-violence. He nevertheless maintains that Christians can still be good citizens, provided that society does not demand they be prepared to kill in times of war.

Hauerwas shares with Ramsey an emphasis upon the centrality of theology within Christian ethics. But this emphasis leads him in a very different way – away from Just War and into radical pacifism. His understanding of pacifism, he insists, is theological, not political or philosophical:

> Pacifism is not just another way that some Christians think they should live. Rather pacifism is the form of life that is inherent in the shape of Christian convictions about God and his relation to us. Though it counts individual passages of scripture such as Matthew 5.38–48 important, pacifism does not derive its sole justification from them. Rather pacifism follows from our understanding of God which we believe has been most decisively revealed in the cross of Jesus Christ. Just as God refused to use violence to insure the success of his cause, so must we (Hauerwas, 1985:99–100).

The Argentinian Methodist **José Míguez Bonino** (1924–2012) is radically different again. Writing from a perspective within **liberation theology**, his 1975 book *Revolutionary Theology Comes of Age* offers an understanding of 'peace' at considerable odds with that of Hauerwas.

Bonino recognises frankly that, at first at least, 'ideas of confrontation, struggle, and violence seem particularly repugnant to the Christian conscience'. Yet as a liberation theologian he does believe that violent struggle is sometimes justifiable.

To reach this position he distinguishes between two different conceptions of 'peace':

> One of them is built on the principle of the rationality of the universe – the conviction that a universal order penetrates the world. Heaven and earth, nature and society, moral and spiritual life seek the equilibrium that corresponds to their rational place, and the preservation of this order is the supreme value ... The other perspective conceives man as a project of liberation that constantly emerges in the fight against the objectifications given in nature, in history, in society, in religion. Man is a creator, and creation is always, in some measure, a violence exerted on things as they are (Bonino, 1975:114).

He argues that both of these conceptions of peace are present in the Bible, yet it is the second that is most prominent, especially within the prophetic tradition. For him, violence within the latter is part of a struggle for justice: 'conflict and violence are means to break out of conditions (slavery, vengeance, arbitrariness, oppression, lack of protection, usurpation) that leave a man, a group of people, or a people unable to be and act as a responsible agent ("as a partner in the covenant") in relation to the others, to things, to God' (1975:117–118).

These three Methodist theologians reach very different ethical conclusions that are not easily reconciled.

However, the Southern Baptist **Glen Stassen** (1936–2014) did pioneer a very practical approach that offers an important point of contact between Just War and pacifist perspectives. Stassen's father was governor of Minnesota and served as a United States delegate at the conference that led to the foundation of the United Nations Organisation. Both father and son were Christian peace activists rather than (more typically for Southern Baptists at the time) anti-abortion or anti-feminist activists.

In his seminal 1992 collection *Just Peacemaking: Ten Practices for Abolishing War*, Stassen gathered together theologians from both Just War and pacifist perspectives who shared a common conviction that peace-making is a key Christian priority. Together they also agreed on a range of practical strategies to promote this priority, including to:

- Support non-violent direct action.
- Take independent initiatives to reduce threat.
- Use cooperative conflict resolution.
- Acknowledge responsibility for conflict and injustice and seek repentance and forgiveness.
- Advance democracy, human rights and religious liberty.
- Foster just and sustainable economic development.
- Work with emerging cooperative forces in the international system.
- Strengthen the United Nations and international efforts for cooperation and human rights.
- Reduce offensive weapons and weapons trade.
- Encourage grassroots peace-making groups.

Of course, this strategy does not resolve theological differences but it might reduce tension between them.

## ANGLICAN POSITIONS ON JUST WAR AND PACIFISM TODAY

Clear differences can also be found among Anglican theologians today.

The Evangelical Anglican theologian **Oliver O'Donovan**, who was supervised as a postgraduate by Paul Ramsey, examines Just War theory in depth in the lead-up to the Iraq War in his 2003 book, *The Just War Revisited*. Like Ramsey he is highly critical of statements on war by some church leaders, with their 'voices raised with perfect foreknowledge around me'.

Ramsey's target, as already seen, are those church leaders who unambiguously condemned American involvement in Vietnam or dismissed nuclear deterrence as evil, whereas O'Donovan's target is (just as controversially) those church leaders who unambiguously condemned British involvement in the Iraq War.

Unlike Welty, the Catholic bishops and even Stassen, O'Donovan does not place much reliance upon the United Nations. Noting its indecisiveness ahead of the Iraq War, he remarks critically that 'the quickest way to make the great UN experiment a memory of past history is to try to use it as an icepack to freeze the nations of the world into inactivity'.

Perhaps this judgment is too focused upon the Iraq War. When the Gulf and Balkan Wars are added, a more mixed, albeit confusing, picture emerges. The first Gulf War was authorised by the United Nations and was halted when the United Nations' mandate expired. In contrast, the Iraq War was not sanctioned by the United Nations because of objections by Russian and French delegates. The bombing of the Balkans was legitimated by NATO rather than by the United Nations – once again Russian delegates objected. Later in the same year it was the turn of the Russians to bomb Grozny in Chechnya without legitimation from the United Nations.

What O'Donovan mainly seeks to do in *The Just War Revisited* is to give greater nuance to the categories that Just War theory deploys. For example, on just intention he argues:

There is, in fact, only one 'just intention' in armed conflict, and that is to distinguish innocence from guilt by overcoming direct co-operation in wrong. To search for a pure intention *behind* this intention is to chase a will o' the wisp. An act of war, like any other act, is inserted into a dense weave of practical purposes and intentions, most of which will inevitably be peculiar to the circumstance and the particular agents (O'Donovan, 2003:42).

Applying this concept of intention to the atomic bombing of Hiroshima, he then claims:

One can test for the intention to harm non-combatants by putting a simple hypothetical question: if it were to chance that by some unexpected intervention of Providence the predicted harm to non-combatants did not ensue, would the point of the attack have been frustrated? If on 6 August 1945 all the citizens of Hiroshima, frightened by a rumour of what was to occur, had fled the city, would the attack have lost its point? If the answer is 'yes', then there was an intention to harm them, and their deaths were not collateral (O'Donovan, 2003:45-46).

The Anglican Christian ethicist **Nigel Biggar**, himself supervised by O'Donovan, goes further, as the title of his 2013 book, *In Defence of War,* suggests. Here he argues that even military belligerence can be justified, although he does add this important qualification:

By 'just war' I do not refer to war that is simply or perfectly just; and I certainly do not refer to a war that is holy. 'Just' here means 'justified' – on balance and all things considered. No war waged by human beings will ever be simply just; but that is not to say that no war can ever be justified (Biggar, 2013:3).

Nevertheless, he also notes:

As I believe in the fact of gross and intractable wickedness, so I believe that punishment is necessary and that it has a basic, broadly retributive dimension. Retribution is important because wrongdoing needs to be contradicted, fended off, and reversed. Not to contradict it and fend it off and try to reverse it is to imply that it does not matter and, therefore, that its victims do not matter ... Human beings are capable of loving what is good and doing what is right, sometimes with heroic courage. Equally, however, they are capable of becoming so wedded to evil that sweet reason, for all its patience, cannot detach them (Biggar, 2013:11–12).

His initial chapter is entitled 'Against Christian pacifism'. In a following chapter he cites at length the war diaries of combatants to show that their motives were often based upon 'love'. Later he says of the Battle of the Somme that 'it was terribly and tragically managed by imperfect generals. But it was not criminally careless, nor was it futile' (2013:146). And towards the end of the book he gives a detailed account of the Iraq War, concluding that, on balance, it was a just war.

Biggar goes further than most Anglican ethicists in attacking Christian pacifism and defending military belligerence. By way of contrast, it is difficult to find an Anglican pacifist theologian who can remotely match the status of the Methodist Stanley Hauerwas (although, it should be noted, Hauerwas is married to an Anglican priest). The Anglican Pacifist Fellowship has existed since the 1930s and still endures, but its membership is relatively small.

The theologian **John Milbank**, the key founder of the theological movement **Radical Orthodoxy**, might be considered an exception. His influential 1990 book (revised in 2006), *Theology and Social Theory*, argues, instructively, that Christianity offers the following ethical counter-narrative to the secular world:

- First, the practice of charity and forgiveness as involving the priority of gratuitous creative giving of existence, and so of difference.
- Second, the reconciliation of difference with virtue, fulfilling true virtue only through reconciliation.
- Third, the treatment of peace as a primary reality and the denial of an always preceding violence (Milbank, 2006:429).

Some have interpreted this to mean that Milbank is a thoroughgoing pacifist. However, this interpretation misses his strong affection for Augustine.

A few pages earlier, Milbank explicitly (and controversially) supports Augustine's use of civil authorities to suppress violently what he regarded as heretical beliefs:

> Augustine admits, correctly in my view, the need for some measures of coercion, in some circumstances, because ... sometimes people can be temporarily blind and will only be prevented from permanent self-damage when they are forced into some course of action, or prevented from another (Milbank, 2006:424).

Given her experience under apartheid, the South African feminist Anglican theologian **Denise Ackermann** might well dissent radically from Milbank at this point. The authorities promoting apartheid did indeed believe they were right to suppress those anti-racist activists whom they regarded as 'heretical'.

Ackermann argues in a 2013 article for people in her country to accept 'difference' – 'difference lies at the heart of the inability of human beings to live together in justice, freedom and peace':

> During those terrible years [under apartheid] in my country when difference was used as category to exclude the majority of people from their rightful place, I learnt the true challenge of 'we who are many are one body for we all partake of the one bread' (1 Corinthians 12:12). Sharing the cup with a homeless person, seeking warmth in the cathedral, with street children who wander in looking for money to spend on bread or glue, with women and men across all racial and class divides, with the Nationalist politician whose ideology I despised, shattered the chains of the apartheid view of difference like a thunderbolt. I continue to remind myself of the power of the 'one cup' as I stand next to the church council member whose sexist attitudes undermine vestry meetings and the cleric who believes that only men may consecrate the meal. I also stand next to the person I know is HIV positive, the father carrying his daughter with tubes coming from her head, the friend who is riddled with cancer and the pregnant woman seeking a blessing for her unborn child (Ackermann, 2013: online).

The situation in South Africa following the collapse of apartheid required **just policies after war** – especially those policies of justice and reconciliation promoted by President Nelson Mandela and Ackermann's fellow-Anglican, Archbishop Desmond Tutu:

> The poisonous apartheid mentality of Afrikaner nationalism, the genocidal activities of the Nazis, the Hutus, and the present regime in Sudan, the intransigent otherness of the Serbs, Bosnians and Croats, militancy of religious fundamentalism and all racist and sexist attitudes, are contemporary examples of otherness as threat (Ackermann, 2013: online).

For Ackermann, 'to be fully human is to live with relatedness' and to live with 'difference'. She finds this expressed in both the South African concept of *ubuntu* (mutual togetherness) and in the Christian doctrines of the Trinity and the Church as the Body of Christ:

> At the Lord's table we are offered the consummate step in forging an ethic of relationship in difference and otherness. This visible, bodily practice of relationship with all its potential for healing is ours. Through the Eucharist our relationship with the Word who became flesh, died on a cross and rose again, offers us relationship with those who are at the altar rail with us and with all who suffer and seek new life (Ackermann, 2013: online).

## CASE-STUDY 2: TRADING WEAPONS OF MASS DESTRUCTION

Mass shootings at schools around the world, and especially in the United States, have raised important ethical questions about the arms trade, gun rights and gun control. Christian principles have been cited by opposing sides in this debate. They are principles that were also cited in the polarised debate about the propriety of nuclear weapons in the previous generation.

**Deterrence** is one of the most widely used concepts when people defend the possession of weapons of mass destruction. In the Cold War between the Soviet Union and the United States (together with the United Kingdom and France) following the Second World War, the doctrine of mutually assured destruction was based upon deterrence. This doctrine held that, because the opposing sides both possessed sufficient nuclear weapons to annihilate whole cities, this deterred either side from actually doing so. Both sides insisted that, whichever side first used such weapons, the other side would immediately respond and both sides would then be devastated.

Some people have used a similar argument to defend the sale of guns to deter mass shootings in schools. They argue that, if schools were heavily defended with guns, would-be perpetrators of mass shootings would be deterred. These would-be perpetrators would be forced to think twice, knowing that they would soon be shot themselves if they attempted a school massacre.

Does deterrence actually work? Defenders of nuclear weapons argue that nuclear deterrence has indeed worked very well. There has, after all, been no use of nuclear weapons in war since 1945. The atom bombs that destroyed Hiroshima and Nagasaki have acted as a lasting deterrent and were, some would argue, entirely justified by doing do.

This is not the place to assess whether deterrence actually works. Social and political scientists need to make that assessment. But it is the place to assess whether 'deterrence' in this context is ethically justified. More specifically, can Christian ethics justify such deterrence?

Some Christian ethicists use a **common good** argument to show that the doctrine of mutually assured destruction contains a disturbing fallacy. In summary form it is this:

- If the mutual possession of nuclear weapons is essential for preserving peace, then all nations should possess them.
- But if all nations do possess them, then the chances of a rogue nation – or of a suicidal faction within a nation – actually using them increases.
- The doctrine encourages nuclear proliferation which, in turn, makes the control of nuclear weapons ever-more difficult.
- The common good of humankind requires nuclear weapons to be in full control and is deeply harmed if they are not.

In short, nuclear deterrence works against the common good. The possession of nuclear weapons may be considered to be in the interest of any particular country but it is not in the interest of the global population.

Another fallacy involves **intention**:

- For the doctrine of mutually assured destruction to work, politicians on both sides must convince their opponents that they will respond in kind to any nuclear attack, even though this will devastate everyone.
- Politicians may have personal qualms about this (and, if they are Christians, surely they should have such qualms).
- But they cannot share these qualms with others, because if they did their nuclear weapons would cease to be a deterrent.
- So politicians in command of nuclear weapons are either lying or they really are prepared to become mass killers.
- And the voting public has no means of telling whether they are deceitful or whether they are murderous.

Many Christian ethicists will regard either prospect as deeply troubling.

They might also have a **principled objection** to deterrence. Some criminologists argue that the very concept of deterrence is unprincipled, since it involves punishing one person more harshly than usual in order to deter other people from acting in the same way. For example, deterrence was often used in the past to justify the gallows in the United Kingdom or the guillotine in France. These deliberately brutal and macabre forms of capital punishment were used on murderers in order to deter other would-be murderers. But even if they did act as such a deterrent (that was often disputed before they were abolished), such executions were both brutal and, of course, irreversible even when there had been a miscarriage of justice.

The American atomic bombing of Hiroshima and Nagasaki and the Allied mass bombing of German civilians in Dresden face a similar principled objection. Many Christian ethicists are highly critical of both – arguing that neither conforms to the two key criteria of just practices within war, namely **proportionality** and **discrimination**. They were not proportionate because they involved massive killing and (for atomic bombs) long-term suffering across generations of Japanese people. And they were not discriminate because they were not aimed at military targets. Instead, civilians were deliberately bombed in order to deter their politicians from continuing the war.

But just suppose, for a moment, that these problems with deterrence are overcome and that most people can agree that the possession of guns in schools (and everywhere else) and nuclear weapons in nations work as effective peacekeepers. Would there still be an ethical problem about trading them?

This scenario probably has more to do with **just policies after war** than just causes for going to war or just practices within war.

Luther, as mentioned earlier, had a surprisingly lax attitude to mercenaries. Provided they were not greedy they could sell their military skills to different rulers. Given that Luther had a low opinion of most rulers, it is remarkable that he did not qualify this advice in some way. Perhaps mercenaries should only sell their skills to rulers they regard as benevolent − just as Nepalese Gurkhas do today. Not only did Luther lack any such qualification, he also insisted that rulers, good or bad, should be obeyed.

So, following Luther, Christian ethicists might similarly argue that, provided they are not greedy, people are free to trade weapons, large or small, for whatever reason they like. Or, more moderately, they might argue that people are free to trade weapons, large or small, purely for peacekeeping purposes. The possibility that non-Christians may use them for non-peacekeeping purposes is a separate issue and need not vex Christians. The latter already know, from Luther, that they are few in number and that the rest of humanity is deeply sinful.

Some of the rhetoric, citing the Second Amendment, about 'the right of people to keep and bear arms' within the United States gun lobby has affinities with this position. It is, however, very far indeed from Denise Ackermann's position on just policies after apartheid − especially those involving *ubuntu* and **reconciliation**. From her perspective as a **feminist theologian**, Christians are not exempt from caring about wider social harms and the effect of policies upon the vulnerable. She would, surely, expect the gun lobby to take full account of the misuse of dangerous weapons, especially when used to massacre school children.

**Liberation, post-colonial** and **womanist** forms of Christian ethics might also note that nuclear weapons are largely possessed by the wealthiest nations on earth, quite a number with an imperial past and/or former links to slave ownership. In this respect North Korea is unusual and, given its strong resentment of capitalist nations, potentially very dangerous. A bias to the poor and vulnerable makes all three of these perspectives within Christian ethics likely to oppose the possession of – let alone the trade in – nuclear weapons.

**Roger Williamson**'s 1992 report, *Profit without Honour? Ethics and the Arms Trade*, written for the British Council on Christian Approaches to Defence and Disarmament, argued that there was a broad consensus emerging across different churches:

> The accumulated evidence of the church statements of the British churches, European churches, the Roman Catholic Church (both centrally and in its national episcopal conferences), as well as international ecumenical bodies presents an increasingly clear voice in favour of bringing the arms trade under stricter control based upon moral principles. There are persistent pleas for greater openness and an insistence that the arms industry should not be allowed to be so dominant that pressure to sell arms overrides ethical considerations (Williamson, 1992:106–107).

Almost three decades later, sadly, it is not clear that much progress has made in this important area. The arms trade flourishes while ethical constraints languish. And other issues, such as climate change and the environment, now receive more attention, even within Christian ethics.

## FURTHER READING

All of the quotations of the following authors in this chapter can be found in greater detail in Section 3 of my *A Textbook of Christian Ethics*:

Aquinas, Thomas (1972), *Summa Theologica*, 2a2ae, 40.1–2 (Vol XXXV of the English Dominican translation, London: Eyre & Spottiswoode, and New York: McGraw-Hill).

Augustine (1956), Reply to Faustus the Manichaean XXII, 69–76 (*The Nicene and Post-Nicene Fathers*, vol IV, Grand Rapids, MI: Eerdmans, trans. R. Stothert).

Hauerwas, Stanley (1983) [1984], *The Peaceable Kingdom* (Notre Dame, IN: University of Notre Dame Press and London: SCM Press)

Hauerwas, Stanley (1985), *Against the Nations* (Minneapolis, MN: Winston Press).

Luther, Martin (1967), Whether Soldiers, too, Can be Saved in *Luther's Works* (Vol 46, Philadelphia: Fortress Press, trans. Charles M. Jacobs and Rev. Robert C.Schulz, pp. 96–99, 104–106, 107–111, 115–116 & 130–132).

Ramsey, Paul (1961), *War and the Christian Conscience* (Durham, NC: Duke University Press).

Ramsey, Paul (1963), *The Limits of Nuclear War* (New York: Council on Religion and International Affairs). Ramsey, Paul (1968), *The Just War* (New York: Scribner, 1968). In this advanced level book he defended the Vietnam War.

US Catholic Bishops (1986), *Economic Justice for All: Pastoral Letter on Catholic Social Teaching and the U.S. Economy* (Washington, DC: CTS). Accessible.

US Catholic Bishops (1988), *Building Peace: A Pastoral Reflection on the Response to 'The Challenge of Peace'* (Washington, DC: CTS). Accessible.

## REFERENCES

Ackermann, Denise M. (2013), 'Living with Difference and Otherness: A Response to the Stories from Canada, Spain and Italy,' in *Regreso y Encuentro – Reflexiones Teológicas*. This accessible article can be found online at: https://www.alboan.org/javier2006/pdf_cs/ackermann_europa canada.pdf (accessed 1/7/19).

Biggar, Nigel (2013), *In Defence of War* (Oxford: Oxford University Press). Fairly accessible.

Bonino, José Míguez (1975), *Revolutionary Theology Comes of Age* (London: SPCK, pp. 107–109, 110–112, 112–114 & 114–118; American title, *Doing Theology in a Revolutionary Situation*, Philadelphia, PA: Fortress Press, 1975). Advanced level.

Cahill, Lisa Sowle (1994), *Love Your Enemies: Discipleship, Pacifism, and Just War Theory* (Minneapolis MN: Fortress Press). Chapter 5 will return to her typically advanced level writings.

Hauerwas, Stanley (1985), 'Pacifism: Some Philosophical Considerations,' in *Faith and Philosophy* (vol 2, no 2, April, pp. 99–104). Fairly accessible.

Milbank, John (2006)[1990], *Theology and Social Theory* (Oxford: Blackwell). Extremely influential but demanding, advanced level.

O'Donovan, Oliver (2003), *The Just War Revisited* (Cambridge: Cambridge University Press, pp. 42–47). Influential Christian ethicist and Emeritus Professor of Moral and Pastoral Theology at Oxford: his writing is typically at advanced level.

Ramsey, Paul (1967), *Who Speaks for the Church? A Critique of the 1966 Geneva Conference on Church and Society* (New York: Abingdon, pp.113–116 & 152–157). Accessible.

Stassen, Glen (ed) (1999), *Just Peacemaking: Ten Practices for Abolishing War* (Cleveland, OH: Pilgrim Press). Accessible.

US Catholic Bishops (1983), *The Challenge of Peace: God's Promise and Our Response: A Pastoral Letter on War and Peace* (Washington, DC: National

Conference of Catholic Bishops, and London: SPCK, paras. 85–121, 331–333 & 338–339) and available online at: http://www.usccb.org/up load/challenge-peace-gods-promise-our-response-1983.pdf. Accessible.

US Methodist Bishops (1986), *In Defence of Creation: The Nuclear Crisis and a Just Peace* (Nashville, TN: Graded Press). Accessible.

Williamson, Roger (1992), *Profit without Honour? Ethics and the Arms Trade* (London: Methodist Publishing House). Accessible but difficult to obtain.

Welty, Eberhard (1963), *A Handbook of Christian Social Ethics*, Vol 2 (Edinburgh: Nelson, pp. 408–415 & 417–421, trans. Gregor Kirstein and Rev. John-Fitzsimons). Fairly accessible.

# THE ENVIRONMENT

At the end of the previous chapter it was noted that – rightly or wrongly – climate change and the environment receive more ethical attention today than the arms trade. Sixty years ago, public protests against nuclear weapons were widespread, whereas now public protests, such as Extinction Rebellion, are more likely to be about the environment.

Christian ethicists (including myself) were quite slow to spot this shift of public concern. The Anglican theologian **Michael Northcott** was an important exception. Responding to the 1992 Rio Declaration on Environment and Development, his 1996 book *The Environment and Christian Ethics* made a major contribution to the discipline, carefully mapping theological responses to global warming (as it was termed then), pollution, soil erosion, deforestation, species extinction and human over-population and over-consumption.

Northcott was also one of the earlier theologians who responded to Lynn White's seminal article 'The Historical Roots of Our Ecologic Crisis', first published in 1967 in the journal *Science*. **Lynn White** (1907–1987) was a medieval historian with a particular interest in evolving forms of technology. He was the son of a Presbyterian professor of Christian ethics, had a theological degree himself in addition to his degrees in history, and he remained a churchgoer as an adult. However, his article is often viewed as an attack upon Christian faith rather than (more accurately) as a critique of certain forms of Christian faith.

In his article White maintains that, although people have long had an impact upon their physical environment, human technology has now generated a major ecological crisis. His central argument is that Western science and technology, themselves shaped by certain Christian understandings of human nature, have been highly destructive of the environment. For example, evolving ploughing technologies in the West, changing from scratching the soil to digging deeply into it, contributed early and significantly to the domination and destruction of nature.

In the West, White argues, the victory of Christianity over paganism had a profound and adverse effect upon attitudes towards nature. A key text is Genesis 1.26:

> Then God said, Let us make humankind in our image, according to our likeness; and let them have dominion over the fish of the sea, and over the birds of the air, and over the cattle, and over all the wild animals of the earth, and over every creeping thing that creeps upon the earth.

Here God's creation and human 'dominion' seem to be linked.

For White, Christianity – especially Western forms of Christianity – is profoundly anthropocentric (i.e., human-centred). Specifically:

> Christianity inherited from Judaism not only a concept of time as non-repetitive and linear but also a striking story of creation. By gradual stages a loving and all-powerful God had created light and darkness, the heavenly bodies, the earth and all its plants, animals, birds, and fishes. Finally, God had created Adam and, as an afterthought, Eve to keep man from being lonely. Man named all the animals, thus establishing his dominance over them. God planned all of this explicitly for man's benefit and rule: no item in the physical creation had any purpose save to serve man's purposes. And, although man's body is made of clay, he is not simply part of nature: he is made in God's image ... Christianity bears a huge burden of guilt (White, 1967: online).

An important Western exception for White is Francis of Assisi. He concludes his highly influential article by commending Francis's radically different attitude towards nature:

> The key to an understanding of Francis is his belief in the virtue of humility – not merely for the individual but for man as a species.

Francis tried to depose man from his monarchy over creation and set up a democracy of all God's creatures. With him the ant is no longer simply a homily for the lazy, flames a sign of the thrust of the soul toward union with God; now they are Brother Ant and Sister Fire, praising the Creator in their own ways as Brother Man does in his ... I propose Francis as a patron saint for ecologists (White, 1967: online).

## AUGUSTINE ON NATURE

In Chapter 2 it was noted in passing that, in *The City of God*, **Augustine** concludes from Genesis 1.26 that God created human beings to have dominion not over other human beings but only over 'irrational' animals. More specifically:

God did not wish the rational being, made in his own image, to have dominion over any but irrational creatures, not human over human, but human over the beasts. Hence the first just humans were set up as shepherds of flocks, rather than as kings of humans, so that in this way also God might convey the message of what was required by the order of nature.

Taken on its own, this paragraph does seem to confirm White's critique: namely that human beings are considered to have 'dominion' over animals and that this is part of the (God created) order of nature. However, in Augustine's *The Literal Meaning of Genesis*, written some two decades before *The City of God*, a rather different approach to Genesis 1.26 is also evident.

Two features of this earlier and, at times, idiosyncratic commentary on the first three chapters of Genesis are particularly interesting when discussing the environment.

The first is that Augustine does not always think that everything in the world serves a purpose for human beings (i.e., anthropocentrism). He takes literally the statement by God to Adam that 'thistles and thorns' are a punishment for his sin in eating the forbidden fruit (Genesis 3.17–18), but he also speculates that thistles and thorns may originally have had a non-human purpose:

the words, 'Thorns and thistles shall it bring forth to you,' if we understand that earth in producing them before the fall did not do so to afflict man but rather to provide proper nourishment for certain animals, since some animals find soft dry thistles a pleasant and nourishing food ... God does not say, 'Thorns and thistles shall it bring forth,' but bring forth to you; that is, they will now begin to come forth in such a way as to add to your labour, whereas formerly they came forth only as a food for other living creatures.

The second feature is that, although Augustine retains a strong sense of this world being sharply divided by competing forces of good and evil (a feature of his youthful Manichaeism), he does still see real beauty in the whole of God's creation – a beauty that includes both humans and animals:

creatures that lose their own proper beauty by sinning can in no way undo the fact that even they, considered as part of a world ruled by God's providence, are good when taken with the whole of creation ... For God is the all-good Creator of beings, but he is the all-just Ruler of creatures who sin. Hence, whenever creatures individually lose their loveliness by sin, nevertheless the whole of creation with them included always remains beautiful.

In both of these (admittedly quirky by modern standards) ways Augustine does seem to reduce a sharp distinction between human beings and other animals and to glimpse something of the inter-relatedness of life within this world.

## AQUINAS ON NATURE

In contrast, **Thomas Aquinas** seems to subordinate animals entirely to human needs. Unambiguously in *Summa Contra Gentiles* – the work that he wrote earlier than *Summa Theologica* – he concludes a discussion of animals with the following claim:

we refute the error of those who claim that it is a sin for human beings to kill brute animals. For animals are ordered to human beings' use in the natural course of things, according to divine providence. Consequently, humans use them without any injustice, either by killing them or by employing them in any other way. For this reason, God said to Noah: 'As the green herbs, I have delivered all flesh to you' [Gen. 9.3].

Aquinas's distinction between **natural law** arguments and **divine command** arguments can be seen clearly here. So, in this instance, he has already argued from 'the natural order of things' and then re-enforces this with an appeal to God's command to Noah.

The natural law argument that precedes this claim is this: rational/intellectual creatures have special meaning since they are free to control their own actions, to know and love God, and to be aware of their special role within God's providence. As a result, intellectual creatures require special providential care, with other created things being subordinated to them. Only the intellectual creature is by nature free, and only God as God is by nature intellectual. Intellectual creatures are thus closest to the divine image.

For Aquinas it is human beings, not animals, who are these intellectual creatures, and among humans it is men who are more rational than women. Other parts of nature are cared for by God for the sake of the intellectual creatures.

The extent of Aquinas's anthropocentrism is especially evident in the reasons he gives for not being cruel to animals. They have nothing to do with pain or distress to the animals themselves. They are solely concerned with the effect of such cruelty upon human beings:

if any statements are found in Sacred Scripture prohibiting the commission of an act of cruelty against brute animals, for instance, that one should not kill a bird accompanied by her young [Deut. 22.6], this is said either to turn the mind of people away from cruelty which might be used on other people, lest a person through practising cruelty on brutes might go on to do the same to other people; or because an injurious act committed on animals may lead to a temporal loss for some person, either for the agent or for another person.

So, on this understanding of natural law, anthropocentrism *and* patriarchy are both considered to be 'natural'. Lynn White's critique does indeed seem particularly apposite here.

## LUTHER ON NATURE

In his *Lectures on Genesis* – delivered in the last decade of his life and recorded by students – **Martin Luther**, too, considers Genesis 1.26. This is the way that he apparently interprets this text (although some allowance must be made for the accuracy of his students):

> Here the rule is assigned to the most beautiful creature, who knows God and is the image of God, in whom the similitude of the divine nature shines forth through his enlightened reason, through his justice and his wisdom. Adam and Eve become the rulers of the earth, the sea, and the air. But this dominion is given to them not only by way of advice but also by express command. Here we should first carefully ponder the exclusiveness in this: no beast is told to exercise dominion; but without ceremony all the animals and even the earth, with everything brought forth by the earth, are put under the rule of Adam, whom God by an express verbal command placed over the entire animal creation.

In this account Luther reaches a similar conclusion to Aquinas, that Adam and Eve are both made in the image of God but that it is Adam who is expressly given dominion by God:

> the woman appears to be a somewhat different being from the man, having different members and a much weaker nature. Although Eve was a most extraordinary creature – similar to Adam so far as the image of God is concerned, that is, in justice, wisdom, and happiness – she was nevertheless a woman. For as the sun is more excellent than the moon (although the moon, too, is a very excellent body), so the woman, although she was a most beautiful work of God, nevertheless was not the equal of the male in glory and prestige.

Chapter 6 will examine more closely the patriarchy evident here in both Aquinas and Luther.

However, where Luther differs from Aquinas is that he believes that, through sin, human beings have largely lost this divine image. For him Adam and Eve both had amazing mental gifts before the Fall, but after the Fall only small differences remain between human beings and other animals.

In addition, he believes that, before the Fall, Adam and Eve would not have eaten meat 'in preference to the delightful fruits of the earth', whereas after the Fall 'for us nothing is more delicious than meat' – resulting in 'leprous obesity' and a lack of 'physical beauty, health and sound state of humours'. These concerns are again thoroughly anthropocentric – they are concerned with human digestion rather than with animal welfare.

## BEYOND AQUINAS AND LUTHER

There is not much for committed environmentalists or feminists today to treasure about Aquinas and Luther's writings here. It is, of course, anachronistic to expect their writings to be relevant to a perception of the detrimental effects of human practice upon the environment that is so recent. Understandings of animal and human intelligence have also changed radically today in ways that would have astonished both Aquinas and Luther.

Augustine alone, with his extraordinary intellectual curiosity, seems to have anticipated at least something nearer to modern sensitivities towards the environment. Yet even he is of only limited positive value for Christian environmentalists today.

However, there is one negative point that does emerge from comparing Augustine, Aquinas and Luther here. It is simply this: White's critique works well on Aquinas, partially on Luther, but poorly on this early writing of Augustine. Aquinas is indeed 'profoundly anthropocentric' in assuming that rational/intellectual faculties are crucial to, and belong uniquely to, human beings (and to men more than women). This assumption devalues, in descending order, women, slaves, small children, babies, adults with late-stage dementia and all non-human animals.

Returning to *The Environment and Christian Ethics*, **Michael Northcott** argues that 'the recovery of an ecological ethic in the modern world requires the recovery of a doctrine of creation, and the worship of a creator who is also redeemer of the creation'. It is *the whole* of creation that needs to be affirmed and not just the part of it that is focused upon human beings. He continues:

> The non-human world ... does not simply consist of matter and sub-human life forms which either have been constructed by chance, or by

a divine being who brings them into being and then places them entirely at the service of humans. Creation is rather the gifted and blessed state of embodied being for which God intends goodness and blessing from the beginning of the cosmos, an intention which is reaffirmed in the coming of Christ and the gift of the Spirit (North-cott, 1996:222).

Specifically on Genesis 1.26, Northcott departs radically from Aquinas's interpretation of 'dominion':

Dominion has frequently been misinterpreted as meaning domination and possession. But the Hebrew root of the verb translated subdue or rule means vice-regent or steward and not ruler. God puts humans over nature not as owner or exploiter but as the steward who shares the creative care of the creator (Northcott, 1996:180).

On anthropocentrism, Northcott is critical of both papal teaching at the time and, in contrast, the radical feminist theologian **Rosemary Radcliffe Ruether**'s adoption of the concept of Gaia. He regards the latter as too inclined towards neo-Paganism and the former as 'implacably opposed to any form of artificial birth control ... opposition [which] has tremendous implications for human population growth, especially in majority Catholic countries in the Third World' (Northcott, 1996:136).

It is now a generation since *The Environment and Christian Ethics* was published, so it is worth taking each of the issues that Northcott identifies separately in this important ethical area. In turn they are: the interpretation of Genesis 1.26 and creation in the Tanakh (Hebrew Bible); anthropocentrism and ecojustice; feminism; and papal teaching. There have been significant developments and tensions within Christian ethics on each of these issues.

## GENESIS 1.26 AND CREATION IN THE TANAKH

The single word 'dominion' that is still used in many modern translations of Genesis 1.26 continues to generate debate. The translation given at the beginning of this chapter comes from the highly regarded New Revised Standard Version of the Bible. It is politically correct in using the word 'humankind' rather than 'mankind' or 'man' to translate the Hebrew word *adam* (as in Adam and Eve), but it has not replaced 'dominion' with, say, 'stewardship'. Humankind (through Adam) is still granted 'dominion over the fish of the sea, and over the birds of the air, and over the cattle, and over all the wild animals of the earth' by God.

The fact remains that specialists in Hebrew are by no means as convinced as Northcott that 'stewardship' is an accurate translation of Genesis 1.26. For them it is perhaps just a misleading attempt to get around a difficult text.

For the philosopher **Stephen R.L. Clark**, a committed Anglican and vegetarian, the very concept of 'stewardship' to depict humankind's relationship to the environment is deeply questionable. Already in his 1993 book, *How to Think About the Earth: Philosophical and Theological Models of Ecology*, Clark writes sharply about 'the fashionable cant of "stewardship"' (Clark, 1993:53), observing that 'many believers, especially at conferences about the duties of "stewardship", *talk* lovingly about God's creatures and the everlasting covenant, and then start eating them' (1993:113).

For Clark the concept of stewardship assumes that human beings are still in control of all other living creatures even if they do not seek to dominate them. In contrast, in an article written seven years earlier, 'Christian Responsibility for the Environment', he depicts a relationship to the environment not so based upon human control:

> If we cannot live in the land on the terms allotted to us, of allowing others their place, not disregarding the needs of the apparently defenceless, not claiming the right to decide how all things should go, then we shall find that we have lost the land. The natural historian of a future age may be able to point to the particular follies that brought ruin – chopping down the tropical rain-forests, meditating nuclear war, introducing hybrid monocultures, spreading poisons, financing grain-mountains and rearing cattle in conditions that clearly breach the spirit of the commandment not to muzzle the ox that treads out the corn (Deut. 28.4) (Clark, 1986:31).

Those evangelical Christians who are committed either to the **prosperity gospel** or to **Adventist** beliefs may be content with 'dominion' in Genesis 1.26. Neither group has shown much interest in ecological issues. For proponents of the prosperity gospel it is human prosperity that is their primary aim (along with human health and human salvation). If that entails domination of the environment, then so be it. Typically for Adventists this world is soon to be destroyed, so fears about climate change and human-induced environmental destruction are largely irrelevant to them.

Both Northcott and Clark tend to present a largely positive take on the Bible's various approaches to the natural world. Clark, for example, writes lyrically as follows:

> No-one who reads the Bible can doubt that its human authors were deeply conscious of the natural world, the creation, the land flowing with milk and honey. Where we see 'nature', the non-human environment ruled by powers alien to humankind, they saw God's creation, a world continually offering embodied images of the spiritual values they pursued. 'The God of Israel spoke, the Rock of Israel spoke of [David]: He who rules men in justice, who rules in the fear of God, is like the light of morning at sunrise; a morning that is cloudless after rain and makes the grass sparkle from the earth' (2 Samuel 26.3f). In the mouths of poets and prophets this is more than simile, more than a rather strained declaration that a just ruler is like the sun after rain. The prophet sees God's liberating justice in the light when God sets His rainbow in the sky 'sign of the covenant between [Himself] and earth' (Genesis 9.14). 'As the hills enfold Jerusalem, so the Lord enfolds His people' (Psalm 128.2) (Clark, 1986:29–30).

However, one influential group of biblical theologians, led by Norman C. Habel in 2000 and known collectively as the **Earth Bible Team**, has attempted a more critical approach to biblical texts. They have established the following independent 'ecojustice principles' in dialogue with ecologists, realising that some biblical texts may support these principles but others not:

1  *The principle of intrinsic worth*: The universe, Earth and all its components have intrinsic worth/value.
2  *The principle of interconnectedness*: Earth is a community of interconnected living things that are mutually dependent on each other for life and survival.

3    *The principle of voice*: Earth is a subject capable of raising its voice in celebration and against injustice.
4    *The principle of purpose*: The universe, Earth and all its components are part of a dynamic cosmic design within which each piece has a place in the overall goal of that design.
5    *The principle of mutual custodianship*: Earth is a balanced and diverse domain where responsible custodians can function as partners, rather than rulers, to sustain a balanced and diverse Earth community.
6    *The principle of resistance*: Earth and its components not only suffer from injustices at the hands of humans, but actively resist them in the struggle for justice.

These principles do give a clear steer. If, on this understanding, Genesis 1.26 contradicts these principles (as principles 1, 2, 5 and 6 appear to do), then it can be set aside. If another text (such as one of those just cited in Clark) supports them, then it can be accepted.

Unsurprisingly this project has been accused by some of **cherry-picking**. Principles derived from another source are used to judge the merits or demerits of conflicting biblical texts.

Yet a studious **contextual** approach may reduce this risk. After all, biblical texts were obviously not written in an age that was experiencing human-induced climate change or, for that matter, the prospect of nuclear war.

But does the third principle of ecojustice relate solely to 'injustice' for people? Or can injustice apply to non-human forms of life as well? In short, is it anthropocentric or, more specifically, is it exclusively anthropocentric?

## ANTHROPOCENTRISM AND ECOJUSTICE

There is an important dilemma here. Some degree of anthropocentrism (i.e., human-centredness) seems inescapable for ethics. After all, ethics is a human activity. No other creature, let alone the natural order as a whole, can articulate (at least in a way that human beings can understand) ethical concerns. The most that human beings can do is to articulate ethical concerns on behalf of non-human realities. This is manifestly a human activity.

Again, ethics can only hope to shape human behaviour specifically as human behaviour. Human beings may, for example, seek to constrain captive male lions from killing the offspring of solitary females and then from forcibly mating with them. But they cannot persuade such male lions that it is ethically wrong for them to do so. Lions do not respond to, or understand, ethical arguments. Ethical argumentation – as far as we know – is an exclusively human undertaking.

Finally, in terms of proportion, ethics for most people is inescapably anthropocentric. Most people consider that there is a huge ethical difference between the Holocaust that exterminated some five million European Jews and exterminating five million malaria-carrying mosquitoes in central Africa.

Simply to label some forms of ethics as 'anthropocentric' is not sufficient. Ethics cannot altogether avoid being anthropocentric. It need not, however, be concerned *solely* with the welfare of human beings. Environmental ethics has a wider remit than human beings, but it does still address issues in ecojustice, such as climate change, that also affect human beings.

Two Indian theologians have made a particularly significant contribution to the connection between a less anthropocentric understanding of ethics and ecojustice: Metropolitan **Paulos Mar Gregorios** (1922–1996) of the Syrian Orthodox Church of Kerala, south India, and **K.C. Abraham** (1936–2016) of the United Church of South India, Professor of Christian Ethics at the United Theological College, Bangalore.

Gregorios was Moderator of the Issue Group at the 6th Assembly of the World Council of Churches in Vancouver in 1983. In his address to this assembly he outlines the threats to the world from nuclear weapons, biotechnology and global injustice:

> The resources and the technology necessary to ensure a decent standard of living to all human beings are now at the disposal of humankind. And yet the number of the millions who do not have access to the means for a life worthy of human beings continues to increase. While enormous amounts of resources and technology are being wasted on pointless military weapons, millions perish from hunger and malnutrition, ignorance and disease (Gregorios, 1983:35).

Addressing this issue theologically, he argues:

> All life is a gift from God. This should not be regarded as a mere preacher's platitude. To acknowledge one's life, as well as that of others, as a sacred gift has enormous consequences for the way we make our decisions on many issues – suicide, war, poverty, injustice, nuclear weapons, and so on. This claim, however, constitutes one of the dilemmas of our modern civilisation which affirms itself, at least at the state level, as secular (Gregorios, 1983:35).

As an Orthodox Christian he characterises life in ways quite different from any secular understanding at five distinct levels:

(a) *God's life*: self-derived, self-sustaining, self-giving, eternal, infinite, not subject to death or disintegration, unmixed with evil, true being, the ground and source of all being, in itself incomprehensible.

(b) *Angelic life*: created, not mixed with evil and therefore not subject to death, and experiencing the presence of God unhindered by the screen of sin.

(c) *Human life*: created, other-derived, other-dependent, mortal, finite, always mixed with evil.

(d) *Sub-human life on earth*: also created and therefore other-derived and other-dependent, mortal, finite, but integrally related to human life.

(e) *Anti-God life*: created, but in rebellion against the purposes of God, interfering with the affairs of humans, discomfited in Christ, but still allowed to be active as a testing ground for freedom, though doomed to destruction (Gregorios, 1983:42–43).

For him: 'All these five levels of life are interconnected and interacting. Any attempt to understand human life in isolation from the other four levels is bound to be both superficial and misleading.' And all five levels are affected by the Incarnation: 'the astounding new gift of God's grace proclaimed in the gospel and acknowledged in the believing community ... The alienation of humanity from God has now been overcome.'

K.C. Abraham, a leading proponent of Marxist-Christian dialogue, makes an even stronger link than Gregorios between ecojustice and **liberation theology**:

> Ecological crisis should be seen as a justice issue. This is a fundamental perspective that distinguishes people's view on ecology from that of the establishment and even of the experts. Political and social justice is linked to ecological health (Abraham, 1993).

He insists that ecological injustice particularly affects poorer countries. They are especially affected by deforestation, unequal partnerships, uneven distribution of natural resources and the rapid depletion of non-renewable resources:

> Ecological crisis has burst upon our consciousness a new awareness about our dependence on earth. We belong to the earth. We share a common destiny with the earth. This has sharply challenged the modern view of reality and demands a revaluation of previously held scales of values (Abraham, 1993).

This, he argues, has important implications for Christian ethics:

> Liberation theologians have forcefully articulated the biblical motif for liberation in Exodus and other passages. Salvation is liberation. But for them particularly because of the immediate context, liberation is primarily political and economic. We today want to affirm that the liberation that is witnessed to in the Bible includes liberation for creation. According to Paul in Romans, the work of the Spirit, Freedom, is extended to the total renewal of creation. Christ's work of redemption extends to the whole universe. Christ, the Lord of history, initiates a process of transformation that moves toward the cosmic release (Eph. 1.1–10 and Col. 1.15–20) (Abraham, 1993:3–14).

## FEMINIST PERSPECTIVES

The radical theological shift envisaged by K.C. Abraham involves both political and conceptual components. Among the latter, language is crucial, especially given the strong patriarchal language and assumptions of both Aquinas and Luther. Over the last generation, feminist Christian ethics has acted as a significant corrective.

One of the most influential feminist contributors on environmental theology has been **Sallie McFague**, now Emeritus Carpenter Professor of Theology at Vanderbilt Divinity School. Her 1982 book, *Metaphorical Theology: Models of God in Religious Language,* helped to reframe the debate within Christian ethics, as did her 1993 book, *The Body of God: An Ecological Theology.*

McFague's 1991 article 'An Earthly Theological Agenda' starts from a similar position to Abraham, arguing that liberation theology should now include all oppressed creatures, as well as planet earth, since everything on this planet is interrelated and interdependent.

From this point of agreement she then moves to the radical agenda that theology needs to deconstruct and reconstruct its central symbols to take account of ecological issues. For her, these symbols should become cosmocentric, rather than anthropocentric, and more prophetic despite the risk of becoming unpopular in the academic world.

She argues that, in the past, there was an overemphasis upon redemption rather than creation. Theology today should instead serve to deepen our sense of complicity in the earth's decay and also promote 'right relations' – relations that include other creatures and the earth itself:

> The encompassing agenda would be to deconstruct and reconstruct the central symbols of the Jewish and Christian traditions in favor of life and its fulfilment, keeping the liberation of the oppressed, including the earth and all its creatures, in central focus. That is so broad, so inclusive an agenda that it allows for myriad ways to construe it and carry it out. It does, however, turn the eyes of theologians away from heaven and toward the earth; or, more accurately, it causes us to connect the starry heavens with the earth (McFague, 1991:12).

To this end she has explored various metaphors for God, including 'mother' and 'friend', and such metaphors for earth as 'God's body' and for human beings as 'earthlings'. She insists that 'theology is an "earthly" affair in the best sense of that word: it helps people to live rightly, appropriately, on the earth, in our home' and that it has an 'obligation to understand human beings and all other forms of life as radically interrelated and interdependent as well as to understand our special responsibility for the planet's well-being'.

McFague's critics have argued that this understanding of theology is both unbiblical and potentially neo-pagan. Her model of the earth as 'God's body' might seem particularly vulnerable to this criticism, since it risks conflating Creator and creation in a less than biblical way. Nevertheless, there is an abundance of explicit and implicit models of God in the Bible (including 'friend' and 'mother'), so others would argue that McFague is simply extending biblical expression creatively.

Writing as a Catholic, **Ursula King**, now Emeritus Professor of Theology and Religious Studies at the University of Bristol, has focused less upon language and more upon inter-religious spirituality. Among her writings are the 1989 book *Women and Spirituality* and the 2011 book *Teilhard de Chardin and Eastern Religions: Spirituality and Mysticism in an Evolutionary World.*

King's 2000 article, 'Rediscovering Fire: Religion, Science and Mysticism in Teilhard de Chardin', explores a different avenue, arguing that it is the work of the Jesuit priest and palaeontologist **Pierre Teilhard de Chardin** (1881–1955) that is particularly needed to inspire a vision of love for the cosmos.

Teilhard de Chardin's book, *The Phenomenon of Man*, was published posthumously in 1959 (having been suppressed by church authorities during his lifetime). Its mystical connections between evolutionary science and theology were particularly popular in the 1960s, but then gradually fell out of fashion. King, however, has sought to revive this interest, believing it is especially relevant to a more ecologically aware age.

King argues that:

> For Teilhard de Chardin, the universe is not simply an object of scientific inquiry. It is a reality passionately loved and embraced, something alive, throbbing, and pulsating with energy and growth. He refers to mother Earth, the *terra mater*, as our matrix and ground. And he refers to the Earth womb from which we grow and in which we have lasting roots; an Earth whose immensity, richness and diversity of life he approached with great reverence and a deep sense of wonder (King, 2000, online).

There are obvious affinities here with Sallie McFague, albeit from a very different, mystical route:

> At the human level, Teilhard de Chardin's world is marked by experiences of suffering and joy, warmth and love, celebration and ecstasy. One has to be attuned to the tonality of his feeling, to the metaphors of fire and music, which he so often uses. He speaks about a note, a melody, a sound, a rhythm that beats for him at the heart of the universe. He also speaks of the spark of fire, the glow, the leaping up of flame, the blaze that sets alive and consumes (King, 2000, online).

For King herself, such 'mysticism of love' is at the centre of religions and is the deepest spring for ethical action within the world:

> Science, religion and mysticism are always closely intertwined in Teilhard de Chardin's thought, for his science is of central significance to a new mysticism of action and a new understanding of the world. This mysticism of action is the mysticism of unification, of bringing everything, all the diverse elements (the cosmic, human, and divine) together. It is a mysticism of transformation and of sanctification, where holiness is understood as wholeness (King, 2000, online).

## AN ONGOING TASK

Compared with the long Christian debate about the ethics of warfare, the debate within Christian ethics about the environment is still in its infancy, albeit with a growing consensus today in favour of both peace-making and environmental sustainability. In contrast, it will be seen in Chapters 5 and 6 that 'status of life' issues (such as abortion and assisted dying) and sexuality issues (especially homosexuality) sharply divide present-day churches.

However, it has been seen that Augustine, Aquinas and Luther are not especially helpful guides for theological responses to the current ecological crisis. Michael Northcott did provide a helpful map for Christian ethics 20 years ago on this important topic, but the debate has moved on since then and, doubtless, will keep moving on.

There is one particular area addressed by Northcott that has changed radically. Two decades ago he was sharply critical of some papal teaching, especially that forbidding effective contraception. It will be seen in Chapter 5 that this Vatican interdiction remains in place. However, **Pope Francis**'s 2015 encyclical on climate change, *Laudato si*, has now made a very significant contribution to environmental ethics.

## CASE-STUDY 3: RAPID CLIMATE CHANGE AND *LAUDATO SI*

At the outset any serious ethical discussion of climate change is faced with two important questions: first, is rapid climate change really happening; and, second, if it is, are human-generated carbon emissions a major contributor to rapid climate change?

These questions need to be answered by qualified scientists and cannot be settled convincingly here. A non-scientist might, though, observe that, even in recent times, scientists have changed tack on global issues (for example, moving from a Steady State to a Big Bang theory of the origins of the universe). Nevertheless, for the moment at least, there does seem to be a growing scientific consensus giving a 'yes' to both of these questions.

Unless this scientific consensus is overturned, it seems prudent for ethicists to take rapid climate change seriously. Global warming (an aspect of climate change) does, after all, have huge implications for species survival – human and non-human – on this planet. In addition, three decades on from the Rio Declaration on Environment and Development there has been depressingly little international political action to reduce human-generated carbon emissions.

*Laudato si* (Praise be to you) are two words taken from Francis of Assisi's *Canticle of the Creatures*: 'Praise be to you, my Lord, through our Sister, Mother Earth, who sustains and governs us, and who produces various fruit with coloured flowers and herbs.'

Pope Francis's 2015 encyclical follows Lynn White in suggesting Francis of Assisi as patron saint of the ecological movement. This passionate encyclical does take rapid climate change very seriously indeed, along with a number of other intertwined global issues, including poverty, pollution, water scarcity, loss of biodiversity and urban unrest. Rapid climate change affects all of these areas:

> Climate change is a global problem with grave implications: environmental, social, economic, political and for the distribution of goods. It

represents one of the principal challenges facing humanity in our day. Its worst impact will probably be felt by developing countries in coming decades. Many of the poor live in areas particularly affected by phenomena related to warming, and their means of subsistence are largely dependent on natural reserves and ecosystemic services such as agriculture, fishing and forestry (Pope Francis, 2015: para. 26).

Pope Francis is clearly aware that his immediate predecessors were criticised by environmentalists for refusing to countenance effective means of contraception. At one point he writes defensively: 'Instead of resolving the problems of the poor and thinking of how the world can be different, some can only propose a reduction in the birth rate' (2015: para. 50). At another point he also raises the issue of abortion:

Since everything is interrelated, concern for the protection of nature is also incompatible with the justification of abortion. How can we genuinely teach the importance of concern for other vulnerable beings, however troublesome or inconvenient they may be, if we fail to protect a human embryo, even when its presence is uncomfortable and creates difficulties? (Pope Francis, 2015: para. 120).

Otherwise he avoids these two issues (to which Chapters 5 and 6 will return) and focuses upon social ethics, showing in the process a clear knowledge of current environmental ethics.

For instance, on 'dominion' in Genesis 1.26 he takes a **contextual approach** and, with only one exception (in para 116), does not typically link dominion to stewardship:

The biblical texts are to be read in their context, with an appropriate hermeneutic, recognizing that they tell us to 'till and keep' the garden of the world (cf. *Gen* 2:15). 'Tilling' refers to cultivating, ploughing or working, while 'keeping' means caring, protecting, overseeing and preserving. This implies a relationship of mutual responsibility between human beings and nature. Each community can take from the bounty of the earth whatever it needs for subsistence, but it also has the duty to protect the earth and to ensure its fruitfulness for coming generations (Pope Francis, 2015: para. 67).

He also offers a sustained critique of anthropocentrism, albeit making a point that is highly relevant to the issue of human action to reduce carbon emissions:

> A misguided anthropocentrism need not necessarily yield to 'biocentrism', for that would entail adding yet another imbalance, failing to solve present problems and adding new ones. Human beings cannot be expected to feel responsibility for the world unless, at the same time, their unique capacities of knowledge, will, freedom and responsibility are recognized and valued (Pope Francis, 2015: para. 118).

However, Pope Francis's most distinctive contribution to the debate on rapid climate change, drawn from Catholic social ethics, involves the principle of **the common good**. Within philosophy, defending the notion that we have an ethical duty towards future generations (i.e., towards 'people' who are not yet 'people') is sometimes thought to be problematic. In contrast, common good arguments in Catholic social ethics – used on such global issues as world peace or climate change – have the following features:

- Common good arguments require us to identify 'goods' that we believe all should share equitably, whatever society we live in or whether or not we have yet to be born.
- Common good arguments may require *all those living now* to reduce their demands (for the sake of future generations).
- Common good arguments do not, therefore, depend upon simply balancing the self-interests of those living.
- Rather, common good arguments seek to evoke altruism, especially among those who are at present most privileged.

Pope Francis expresses this as follows:

> Underlying the principle of the common good is respect for the human person as such, endowed with basic and inalienable rights ordered to his or her integral development. It has also to do with the overall welfare of society and the development of a variety of intermediate groups, applying the principle of subsidiarity. Outstanding among those groups is the family, as the basic cell of society. Finally, the common good calls for social peace, the stability and security

provided by a certain order which cannot be achieved without particular concern for distributive justice; whenever this is violated, violence always ensues. Society as a whole, and the state in particular, are obliged to defend and promote the common good (Pope Francis, 2015: para. 157).

The principle of the common good clearly requires a high level of altruistic commitment. Following an approach in **virtue ethics**, Pope Francis emphasises the need for 'ecological education' and for nourishing ecological virtues within families. For him these virtues also need to be nourished by an **ecological spirituality** across different religious traditions:

A commitment this lofty cannot be sustained by doctrine alone, without a spirituality capable of inspiring us, without an 'interior impulse which encourages, motivates, nourishes and gives meaning to our individual and communal activity'. Admittedly, Christians have not always appropriated and developed the spiritual treasures bestowed by God upon the Church, where the life of the spirit is not dissociated from the body or from nature or from worldly realities, but lived in and with them, in communion with all that surrounds us (Pope Francis, 2015: para. 216).

But will all of this be sufficient to persuade countries around the world to reduce carbon emissions? Rich countries need to be persuaded greatly to reduce their consumption. Poor countries need to be persuaded not to aspire to the levels of consumption of rich nations. Pope Francis sees that market forces push both sets of countries in the opposite direction and that it is unrealistic to expect technology to 'fix' carbon emissions effectively.

He also calls for international sanctions to enforce political promises to reduce carbon emissions, but warns that democratic elections encourage politicians to be more concerned with local, short-term issues than with global, long-term concerns such as climate change. He even admits that the principles aimed at limiting greenhouse gas concentrations in the atmosphere, which the 1992 Rio Declaration 'proclaimed', regrettably 'still await an efficient and flexible means of practical implementation' (2015: para. 167).

There remains a worrying gap here between altruistic, even spiritual, aspirations and socio-political achievements.

## FURTHER READING

All of the quotations of the following authors in this chapter can be found in greater detail in Section 4 of my *A Textbook of Christian Ethics*:

Abraham, K.C. (1992), *Eco-Justice: A New Agenda for Church's Mission* (Bombay: Bombay Urban Industrial League for Development).

Aquinas, Thomas (1975), *Summa Contra Gentiles* 3.2.112–113 (London: University of Notre Dame Press, andNew York: Doubleday, trans. Vernon J. Bourke, pp. 114–119).

Augustine (1982), *De Genesi ad Litteram* (The Literal Meaning of Genesis, New York: Newman Press, trans. JohnHammond TaylorS.J., ch. 18–24, pp. 93–102).

Clark, Stephen R.L. (2000), *Biology and Christian Ethics* (Cambridge: Cambridge University Press). This book for the New Studies in Christian Ethics series is demanding and at an advanced level.

King, Ursula (1989), *Women and Spirituality* (New York: New Amsterdam Books).

King, Ursula (2011), *Teilhard de Chardin and Eastern Religions: Spirituality and Mysticism in an Evolutionary World* (Mahwah, NJ: Paulist Press).

Luther, Martin (1958), Lectures on Genesis in *Luther's Works* (Vol 1, Concordia Publishing House, ed. Jaroslav Pelikan, trans. George V. Schick, pp. 66–73).

McFague, Sallie (1982), *Metaphorical Theology: Models of God in Religious Language* (Minneapolis, MN: Fortress Press). McFague, Sallie (1993), *The Body of God: An Ecological Theology* (Minneapolis, MN: Fortress Press).

Northcott, Michael (2007), *A Moral Climate: The Ethics of Global Warming* (London: DLT, and Maryknoll, NY: Orbis). This is an accessible book.

## REFERENCES

Abraham, K.C. (1993), 'A Theological Response to Ecological Crisis,' in *Bangalore Theological Forum* (XXV:1, March, pp. 3–14). Abraham, K.C. (1993), *Eco-Justice: A New Agenda for Church's Mission* (Bombay: Bombay Urban Industrial League for Development, 1992). Accessible.

Clark, Stephen R.L. (1986), 'Christian Responsibility for the Environment,' in *Modern Churchman* (28:2, pp. 24–31).

Clark, Stephen R.L. (1993), *How to Think About the Earth: Philosophical and Theological Models of Ecology* (London: Mowbray). This is an accessible book.

Gregorios, Paulos Mar (1983), 'Life from the Perspective of Science and the Christian Faith,' in William H. Lazareth (ed), *The Lord of Life* (Geneva: World Council of Churches, pp. 34–36 & 39–43). Accessible.

Habel, Norman C. (ed) (2000), *Readings from the Perspective of the Earth* (Sheffield: Sheffield Academic Press). Advanced level.

King, Ursula (2000), 'Rediscovering Fire: Religion, Science and Mysticism in Teilhard de Chardin,' in *Earth Light Library: The Magazine of Spiritual Ecology* (Issue 39, Fall). Available online at: https://earthlight.org/essay39_king.html (accessed 30/10/19). Advanced level.

McFague, Sallie (1991), 'An Earthly Theological Agenda,' in *The Christian Century* (108:1, 2–9 January, pp. 12–15). Fairly accessible.

Northcott, Michael (1996), *The Environment and Christian Ethics* (Cambridge: Cambridge University Press). This influential and reasonably accessible book is part of the New Studies in Christian Ethics series.

Pope Francis (2015), *Laudato si*. Can be found online at: https://laudatosi.com/watch. It is very accessible.

Rio Declaration on Environment and Development (1992), can be found online at: https://www.cbd.int/doc/ref/rio-declaration.shtml (accessed 24/7/19).

Ruether, Rosemary Radcliffe (1994), *Gaia and God* (New York: HarperCollins) and *Goddesses and the Divine Feminine* (Berkeley, CA: California University Press, 2005). Advanced level. Chapter 5 considers some of her other writings.

White, Lynn Townsend, Jr (1967), 'The Historical Roots of Our Ecologic Crisis,' in *Science* (155:3767, 10 March, pp. 1203–1207). Available online at: http://www.cmu.ca/faculty/gmatties/lynnwhiterootsofcrisis.pdf (accessed 30/10/19). Accessible.

# 5

# EUTHANASIA AND ABORTION

Personal issues arising from the beginning and ending of human life have proved particularly contentious within Christian ethics in the 21st century. Catholic teaching on contraception has been widely criticised by other churches. Across denominations, homosexual practice has sharply divided Christians. The legalising of induced abortion in many countries, and of voluntary euthanasia in some, has generated sharp debates. So-called 'status of life' issues in this generation threaten the unity of denominations more than, say, the propriety of nuclear weapons – a social issue that divided an earlier generation.

## STATUS OF LIFE ISSUES

**Alasdair MacIntyre**'s seminal 1981 book *After Virtue* – a book that, as noted in Chapter 1, has deeply influenced Christian (and some secular) ethicists – argues that the problem with 'status of life' debates is that they tend to be incommensurable. By this he means that proponents of, say, strong pro-life or pro-choice positions on abortion simply argue across each other with no possibility of ever reaching a consensus. To be blunt: they both *know* that they are right.

This is probably true of many of those who are strongly opposed to, or in favour of, legalised physician-assisted suicide. Those opposed typically *know* that this is murder. Those in favour *know* that this is about personal autonomy. Both sides bolster their arguments with appeals to compassion and to family anecdotes. Of course, many do so because they care. They care passionately.

This incommensurable dichotomy is evident within both Christian and secular forms of ethics. Status of life issues, concerned with vexed issues at the beginning and end of life, do seem to evoke this dichotomy and leave little or no room for consensus.

The feminist Catholic ethicist **Lisa Sowle Cahill** in her 2003 article 'Bioethics, Theology and Social Change' makes the important point that one of the problems is that today:

> For public debate in law, policy, medicine and research, the focal issue is undoubtedly the protection of autonomy by procedural guarantees of informed consent. Meanwhile, religion is framed as entirely pre-occupied with 'status of life' issues, especially the fate of embryos and the processes of reproduction, and as in the grip of a vaguely articulated and ultimately baseless fear that interference with 'natural' reproduction will denigrate 'human dignity.' Leaving aside the possible merit of such concerns, an equally or more important concern of religion and theology – the economics of biotech development and genomics and their effects on social solidarity and distributive justice – is quite effectively kept off the policy table by the dominant discourse, and its construction of 'mainstream' and 'marginal' voices (Cahill, 2003:378–379).

In Chapter 4 it was noted that Pope Francis's encyclical, *Laudato si*, makes reference to the issues of contraception and abortion – affirming the traditionalist Catholic teaching on both – but it does not dwell upon either issue. Evidently his concern is to encourage consensus on the social issues of climate change and environmental sustainability, realising that the more personal issues of contraception and abortion are unlikely to produce consensus (even among Catholic laypeople).

Reaching consensus on 'status of life' issues is not the aim of this or of the next two chapters. More modestly, their aim is to map some of the current tensions within Christian ethics on a range of interpersonal issues and to trace ongoing critical connections with Augustine, Aquinas and Luther's concerns.

## AUGUSTINE ON SUICIDE

There is an obvious link between suicide and euthanasia, especially when the latter is defined as physician-assisted suicide ('suicide' meaning literally 'self-killing'). Until the 1960s attempting to commit suicide was illegal in Britain and most other countries in the West (Switzerland, unusually, never did criminalise suicide). The Suicide Act 1961 decriminalised suicide in England and Wales. Politicians and Anglican bishops at the time argued that it was inhumane to imprison someone who had attempted, but failed, to commit suicide. Many churches also concluded that it was inhumane for them to refuse to bury those who successfully committed suicide. Arguably, decriminalisation did not make suicide a human right since, if it were a right, no one would have a duty to attempt to dissuade someone from committing suicide. It was an act of **compassion** towards vulnerable people who have tried unsuccessfully to commit suicide. Nor did it allow people to help someone else to commit suicide.

However, many in the West today argue that a similar act of compassion should be extended to those suffering from intolerable and untreatable pain. Doctors should, they argue, be allowed to offer them the means to commit suicide – in other words, physician-assisted suicide. Starting with the Netherlands in the 1970s a number of countries in the West, and states within the US and Australia, have come to accept this argument – either deciding not to prosecute doctors who act compassionately or removing legislation that prohibits physician-assisted suicide.

How might **Augustine** have reacted to this argument? After all, it was seen in Chapter 3 that he (and Bishop Ambrose before him) moved away from long-standing Christian opposition to warfare, arguing that it can be justified if authorised by God or by a ruler appointed by God. Might he have agreed with legalising physician-assisted suicide on compassionate grounds?

His discussion of suicide in *The City of God* suggests he would not.

Augustine compares and contrasts Christian and pagan attitudes to suicide, taking the classical story of Lucretia as an example. Should a woman commit suicide in order to avoid either rape or the shame of having been raped? He admits at the outset that: 'Some women killed themselves to avoid suffering anything and surely any man of compassion would be ready to excuse the emotions which led them to do this.'

However, he swiftly concludes that such compassion is misplaced: 'For it is clear that if no one has a private right to kill even a guilty man (and no law allows this), then certainly anyone who kills himself is a murderer, and is the more guilty in killing himself the more innocent he is of the charge on which he has condemned himself to death.'

The word 'private' in this sentence is crucial. Suicide for Augustine is typically private (in other words, unauthorised) and, therefore, simply murder – murder of oneself.

Nor is he convinced that suicide to avoid the 'pollution' of rape is justified – arguing that 'there will be no pollution if the lust is another's'. In remarkably modern terms, he maintains that the pollution here lies in the mind of the rapist and not in the mind of the woman who has been raped. So, for Augustine, the pagan Lucretia was misguided:

> Her killing of herself because, although not adulterous, she had suf-fered an adulterer's embraces, was due to the weakness of shame, not to the high value she set on chastity. She was ashamed of another's foul deed committed on her, even though not with her, and as a Roman woman, excessively eager for honour, she was afraid that she should be thought, if she lived, to have willingly endured what, when she lived, she had violently suffered.

For Lucretia, 'shame' was key. In contrast, Christian women, Augustine argues, have behaved quite differently:

> When they were treated like this they did not take vengeance on themselves for another's crime. They would not add crime to crime by committing murder on themselves in shame because the enemy had committed rape on them in lust. They have the glory of chastity within them, the testimony of their conscience. They have this in the sight of God, and they ask for nothing more.

So, compared with his position on warfare, Augustine seems to take an absolutist position on suicide. For him suicide is self-murder and is, therefore, not a justifiable way to avoid shame or suffering.

Yet he is aware of biblical precedents that do not appear to fit this absolutist position:

> When Abraham was ready to kill his son, so far from being blamed for cruelty he was praised for his devotion; it was not an act of crime,

but of obedience. One is justified in asking whether Jephtha is to be regarded as obeying a command of God in killing his daughter, when he had vowed to sacrifice to God the first thing he met when returning victorious from battle. And when Samson destroyed himself, with his enemies, by the demolition of the building, this can only be excused on the ground that the Spirit, which performed miracles through him, secretly ordered him to do so.

Samson here is particularly interesting because he apparently commits both suicide and murder. Strikingly, Samson is the nearest thing to a suicide-bomber in the Bible.

Does Augustine really justify this?

His ground for doing so is again based upon **divine command**; the Spirit of God 'secretly ordered him to do so'. To modern eyes, as mentioned in Chapter 3, this argument from silence probably seems remarkably unconvincing. Yet it does raise the possibility that, *if* physician-assisted is legalised (and, therefore, carried out under authority), it *might* then be justifiable in terms of Christian ethics.

The radical Catholic Swiss theologian **Hans Küng** is unusual within Christian ethics for adopting something akin to this position. It may be significant that, although he has worked and lived in Germany for much of his life, Küng is Swiss. As mentioned, his native country, uniquely in Europe, never did criminalise (physician-assisted) suicide. So clinics there are allowed to practise physician-assisted suicide without fear of prosecution.

Writing with his friend, the literary historian Walter Jens (1923–2013), Küng argues in their 1995 book, *A Dignified Dying?*, that physician-assisted suicide should be allowed on compassionate grounds. He admits at the outset that the agonising death of his brother from an inoperable brain tumour, while still in his twenties, strongly influenced his ethical stance: 'Since then I have kept asking myself whether this is the death that God gives, that God ordains. Must men and women "submissively" accept this, too, till the end as "God-given", "divinely willed", even "pleasing to God"?' (Küng & Jens, 1995:24).

Küng distances himself both from traditionalist Catholic teaching (that human life is God-given and therefore inviolable) and from the secular position of the philosopher Peter Singer (that those with a 'definitive loss of consciousness' become 'non-persons').

Instead he argues for a mid-position 'between an anti-religious libertinism without responsibility ("unlimited right to voluntary death") and a reactionary rigorism without compassion ("even the intolerable is to be borne in submission to God as given by God")'.

He justifies this as follows:

> As a Christian and a theologian I am convinced that the all-merciful God, who has given men and women freedom and responsibility for their lives, has also left to dying people the responsibility for making a conscientious decision about the manner and time of their deaths. This is a responsibility which neither the state nor the church, neither a theologian nor a doctor, can take away. This self-determination is not an act of arrogant defiance of God; just as the grace of God and human freedom are not exclusive, neither are God's predestination and human self-determination. In this sense, self-determination is demarcation over against others: just as no one may urge, necessitate or compel others to die, so too no one may compel them to continue to live (Küng & Jens, 1995:37).

There are two important features of Küng's ethical argument in favour of physician-assisted suicide here: one is based upon personal autonomy and the other upon compassion. Augustine might well have disagreed with both.

It has just been seen that, while he recognises the **call of compassion** in some cases of suicide, Augustine insists that this should not be used to justify self-murder. Only a divine command can do that and, in that instance, suicide (such as that of Samson) is no longer to be considered self-murder.

The concept of **personal autonomy** in ethics may also be alien to Augustine's position. In recent times personal autonomy has become a key component of medical ethics and law in Western democratic societies. It is now widely accepted that if patients with capacity refuse to have life-sustaining treatment (including food and water), then they cannot legally or ethically be forced to have that treatment. So, for example, adult Jehovah's Witnesses who have capacity cannot be forced to have a life-saving blood transfusion against their will.

On both of these issues Augustine's position is out of step with beliefs that are widely held today. In the modern debate about physician-assisted suicide, defenders and critics alike tend to use arguments based upon **compassion**. Those following Küng point to compassion for patients who experience intolerable and life-limiting pain or discomfort. Those opposed to Küng typically point to compassion for other vulnerable people who may feel pressurised or even endangered by a change in the law. *Both* sides typically use compassionate anecdotes to support their arguments.

Again, arguments based upon personal autonomy do not necessarily resolve this current debate. Both sides might agree that patients do have a right not to be given treatment against their will. So, forcing adult Jehovah's Witnesses to have a life-saving blood transfusion might indeed save their lives but (in terms of their beliefs) it would also, and disastrously, prevent them from being allowed to enter Heaven.

Even so, it is not clear that this right can be extended without ambiguity into expecting doctors to help patients actually to take their lives. American and British opinion polls suggest that doctors are distinctly less enthusiastic than the general public about legalising physician-assisted suicide. Seven out of ten of those responding to a June 2019 American Medical Association poll agreed that allowing doctors to help patients to die is 'fundamentally incompatible with the physician's role as a healer, would be difficult or impossible to control, and would pose serious societal risks'. Doctors apparently see this role as in conflict with their healing ethos, and perhaps they fear it would put pressure upon their most vulnerable patients. Some patients might even feel it was their duty to have their lives ended to stop them from becoming a financial or social burden upon their families.

However, one point against Küng's argument seems more decisive. A central theological argument against (physician-assisted) suicide is based upon the belief that human life is 'God-given' and therefore inviolable. This is a belief shared by many Jews, Christians and Muslims.

Yet he counters this point with two additional arguments. The first is that this principle has not always been applied to capital punishment (consistent papal opposition to that is fairly recent). The second he puts in the form of a question: 'Why should I not be able to give my life back into God's hands after a mature examination of my conscience?' Indeed, gifts that bind the recipient to the giver (for example, a bride dowry) are typically not seen as genuine 'gifts' at all.

In effect Küng introduces an argument here that produces further ambiguity to this ongoing debate. And, for good measure, he adds a critical reference to papal teaching on contraception (which he opposed vigorously in the 1960s):

> As a believer I know that the life of God is a gift, but I also know that at the same time it is a human responsibility (first of my parents and then my own). One cannot simply 'leave everything to God' at the end of one's life, any more than one can at the beginning. And just as the Roman teaching on birth control has led into a cul-de-sac, so too has its teaching on help in dying (Küng & Jens, 1995:120–121).

## CASE-STUDY 4: RECRIMINALISING ABORTION

With the crucial 1973 decision of the Supreme Court that decriminalised abortion across the United States, following the 1967 Abortion Act in England and Wales making medically induced abortion legal in certain circumstances (and similar moves in many other Western countries), legal abortions have now been practised widely in the West for more than a generation. In the 1950s and 1960s there was widespread discussion within Western churches about the ethics of abortion. The official position of the Catholic Church has remained implacably opposed to induced abortion, as has that of many Orthodox bishops and some leaders within evangelical churches. However, many other denominations have ceased to debate the ethics of abortion and have come to accept that legalised abortion is preferable to any return to the septic deaths of women who resorted to an illegal abortion. Few of these denominations now regard (early) abortion as murder.

Recently, however, there have been a number of attempts by Catholics and Evangelicals, especially in the United States but also in parts of Europe, to reverse laws permitting abortion. In effect they are seeking to recriminalise abortion. What are the ethical arguments for and against this move?

The clearest position is taken by those who have a strongly **principled** approach to abortion. They typically argue that, at conception, a new, unique person is created with the conjoining of the DNA from both the mother and the father. Conceived life is God-given and a part of God's creation. Abortion, at any stage after conception, is murder, and, as such, it breaks one of the Ten Commandments and is always deeply wrong and sinful.

The strength of this position is that it gives a very clear answer to the question: 'when does personhood start?' The answer is unambiguous: 'at conception.' It takes account of **natural law** – regarding the natural conjoining of DNA as crucial – and Christian exponents also tend to cite **biblical** evidence, such as Psalm 139.13–14: 'For it was you who formed my inward parts; you knit me together in my mother's womb. I praise you, for I am fearfully and wonderfully made. Wonderful are your works; that I know very well.'

Christian critics, however, make a number of points against this strongly principled approach to abortion:

- Christian tradition has not always been consistent about regarding conception as the start of personhood. Aquinas, following Aristotle and Augustine, thought that 'animation' or 'ensoulment' came later in a pregnancy. Others (before the discovery of DNA) thought that semen was seed (and the womb simply an incubator) and that deliberately spilling this seed amounted to murder (and, thus, that all forms of contraception were murder). Chapter 6 will return to this point.
- We now know that a majority of human conceptions are spontaneously aborted. It seems odd, then, to conclude that a majority of persons are never actually born and even odder to imagine that Heaven is mostly populated by the unborn.
- While Psalm 139 is important, it does not actually specify when exactly a person is 'knit together' in the womb – nor does any other verse within the Bible.

Those Christians who defended the legalisation of abortion in the 1960s and 1970s often appealed to **virtues** such as compassion and justice. They argued it was unjust that women who had, for example, been raped should be forced to continue with their pregnancies. They were also appalled by those septic deaths of women caused by illegal and untrained abortionists in the 1950s – arguing, on **compassionate** grounds, that legalised abortion, however distasteful some might find it, would make such abortionists redundant (as indeed it largely has). Recriminalising abortion would, they argue, risk a return of these illegal and dangerous abortions.

Principled opponents of abortion who now campaign to recriminalise abortion often respond as follows: the whole focus here is upon the woman seeking an abortion and *not* upon the unborn child. Even if a woman is raped, that does not give her an ethical justification for murdering the child within her.

There is probably no way to reconcile these radically different perspectives – Alasdair MacIntyre does seem to have been right. However, the campaign by some Christians to recriminalise abortion raises, once again, some of the sharp divisions outlined in Chapter 2. It is one thing for Christians to hold and abide by strong principles for themselves, but it is another for them to seek to impose these principles upon others. Previous Evangelical campaigns against alcohol, say, or in favour of censorship within theatres, sought to do just that, but are seldom regarded highly within the West today. If any attempt to recriminalise abortion were to succeed it might face a similar problem. Seeking to impose private morality upon whole populations – as happened within medieval Christendom and still happens within some Islamic states – is regarded within most democracies today as being both repressive and counter-productive.

## FURTHER READING

All of the quotations of the following authors in this chapter can be found in greater detail in Section 5 of my *A Textbook of Christian Ethics*:

Augustine (1972), in David Knowles (ed), *The City of God*, I.17–18, 19b–22 & 27 (London: Pelican Classics, trans. Henry Bettenson, pp. 26–28, 30–34 & 38–39).

Cahill, Lisa Sowle (2004), *Bioethics and the Common Good* (Milwaukee, WI: Marquette University Press). Advanced.

Cahill, Lisa Sowle (2005) *Theological Bioethics* (Washington, DC: Georgetown University Press). Advanced.

## REFERENCES

Cahill, Lisa Sowle (2003), 'Bioethics, Theology and Social Change,' in *Journal of Religious Ethics* (31:3, pp. 366–371, 378–379 & 385–386).

Küng, Hans & Jens, Walter (1995), *A Dignified Dying?* (London: SCM Press, andNew York: Continuum, trans. John Bowden, pp. 24–27, 37–38, 114–116, 116–117, 118–121). Accessible.

MacIntyre, Alasdair (1981), *After Virtue: A Study in Moral Theory* (London: Duckworth. Revised 1985). For more details of this important book see the References in Chapter 1.

# 6

# SEXUALITY AND MARRIAGE

Chapter 4 noted that, in *Summa Contra Gentiles*, **Thomas Aquinas** used a natural law argument to reach the following conclusion:

> Intellectual creatures have special meaning since they are free to control their own actions, to know and love God, and to be aware of their special role within God's providence. As a result, intellectual creatures require special providential care, with other created things being subordinated to them. Only the intellectual creature is by nature free, and only God as God is by nature intellectual. Intellectual creatures (basically human beings) are thus closest to the divine image *and*, among humans, it is men who are more rational than women.

This egregious (to modern sensibilities) conclusion about gender needs to be put into the context of Aquinas's natural law arguments about sexual intercourse and marriage – especially since they have been so crucial to recent papal teaching on sexuality.

## AQUINAS ON SEXUALITY

In *Summa Contra Gentiles* Aquinas starts from a position that appears to be almost modern:

> Suppose there is a woman who is not married, or under the control of any man, either her father or another man. Now, if a man performs the sexual act with her, and she is willing, he does not injure her, because she favours the action and she has control over her own

body. Nor does he injure any other person, because she is understood to be under no other person's control. So, this does not seem
to be a sin.

Of course, this is not quite modern. It still seems to assume that a
woman *is* typically under the control of a man. Yet it appears to
take seriously a libertarian argument widely used today, namely
that, if an action does not harm other people, then an individual
should be free to pursue it.

However, it immediately becomes evident that this is not at
all what Aquinas thinks. He opens his counter argument by
considering the natural function of male semen. Arguably this
is not as sexist as it might seem since – knowing nothing
about the female ovum, let alone the conjoining of both male
and female DNA at conception – he and his contemporaries
simply assumed that semen was the self-contained seed of
human life. The male transmits this human life to the female
for her to incubate.

Unlike all other bodily emissions, semen is not waste material
but the generator of life:

> Therefore, the emission of semen ought to be so ordered that it will
> result in both the production of the proper offspring and in the
> upbringing of this offspring. It is evident from this that every emis-
> sion of semen, in such a way that generation cannot follow, is con-
> trary to the good for man. And if this be done deliberately, it must be
> a sin. Now, I am speaking of a way from which, *in itself* generation
> could not result; such would be any emission of semen apart from
> the natural union of male and female. For which reason, sins of this
> type are called *contrary to nature*. But, if by accident generation cannot
> result from the emission of semen, then this is not a reason for it
> being against nature, or a sin; as for instance, if the woman happens
> to be sterile.

Once again, this is not modern biology. Aquinas makes no mention here of male sterility. Yet the logic is clear: the natural function of something (in this case semen) can, he believes, give clear
ethical directives.

He continues to apply this logic to marriage:

> Likewise, it must also be contrary to the good for man if the semen be emitted under conditions such that generation could result but the proper upbringing would be prevented. We should take into consideration the fact that, among some animals where the female is able to take care of the upbringing of offspring, male and female do not remain together for any time after the act of generation. This is obviously the case with dogs. But in the case of animals of which the female is not able to provide for the upbringing of offspring, the male and female do stay together after the act of generation as long as is necessary for the upbringing and instruction of the offspring ... Now, it is abundantly evident that the female in the human species is not at all able to take care of the upbringing of offspring by herself, since the needs of human life demand many things which cannot be provided by one person alone.

Unfortunately (again, in terms of modern sensibilities) Aquinas's patriarchal assumptions then spoil this argument:

> Again, we must consider that in the human species offspring require not only nourishment for the body, as in the case of other animals, but also education for the soul ... Moreover, a long time is needed for this instruction. Then, too, because of the impulsion of the passions, through which prudent judgment is vitiated, they require not merely instruction but correction. Now, a woman alone is not adequate to this task; rather, this demands the work of a husband, in whom reason is more developed for giving instruction and strength is more available for giving punishment.

On a more positive note, there are other features of Aquinas's views on marriage that chime better with modern sensibilities. He writes about the importance of friendship within marriage, about fathers being concerned about their children, and about sexual intercourse (within an abiding marriage) being good. For him, in contrast to Augustine, sexual intercourse is a natural and God-given phenomenon and therefore cannot be evil in itself. It is only in the wrong context that sexual intercourse is not good.

So what exactly is this wrong context? For Aquinas is it simply sexual intercourse outside marriage?

Evidently not. Aquinas's clear teaching is that 'every [deliberate] emission of semen, in such a way that generation cannot follow ... must be a sin'. On this account, male masturbation and any form of contraception, even within marriage, must be a sin. Indeed, it must be a very serious sin if the male semen is seen as the self-contained seed of human life. It may even be murder.

**Pope Paul VI**'s 1968 encyclical, *Humanae Vitae*, does avoid this conclusion about murder. Catholic natural law teaching had already adjusted to modern biology, realising that male semen is not the self-contained seed of human life. So the deliberate emission of semen 'in such a way that generation cannot follow' could no longer be regarded as murder.

By the late 1960s it was widely assumed that a new encyclical would also adjust to the fact that, in an overpopulated world, many Western Catholics were already using barrier or hormonal contraception within their marriages. *Humanae Vitae* proved them – and Hans Küng – wrong.

This highly significant, and strongly contested, encyclical opens by recognising: the 'rapid growth' of world population 'with the consequence that many families and developing countries are being faced with greater hardships'; 'the new understanding of the dignity of woman, and her place in society'; and new forms of technology. As a result, Paul VI asks:

> Granted the conditions of life today and taking into account the relevance of married love to the harmony and mutual fidelity of husband and wife, would it not be right to review the moral norms in force till now, especially when it is felt that these can be observed, only with the gravest difficulty, sometimes only by heroic effort? (Pope Paul VI, 1968: para. 3).

Addressing this question, he argues that, whatever changes are happening in society, there are abiding features of faithful marriage that apply to any age. In particular, there is 'the inseparable connection, established by God, which man on his own initiative may not break, between the unitive significance and the procreative significance which are both inherent to the marriage act'. Or, to put this into more ordinary language, every act of sexual intercourse should help a couple's mutual intimacy *and* offer the possibility of new life being formed:

> And if each of these essential qualities, the unitive and the procrea-
> tive, is preserved, the use of marriage fully retains its sense of true
> mutual love and its ordination to the supreme responsibility of par-
> enthood to which man is called. We believe that our contemporaries
> are particularly capable of seeing that this teaching is in harmony with
> human reason (Pope Paul VI, 1968: para. 12).

From this he draws the following conclusions:

> Therefore we base our first principles of a human and Christian doc-
> trine of marriage when we are obliged once more to declare that the
> direct interruption of the generative process already begun and, above
> all, direct abortion, even for therapeutic reasons, are to be absolutely
> excluded as lawful means of controlling the birth of children. Equally
> to be condemned ... is direct sterilisation, whether of the man or of
> the woman, whether permanent or temporary. Similarly excluded is
> any action, which either before, at the moment of, or after sexual
> intercourse, is specifically intended to prevent procreation – whether
> as an end or as a means (Pope Paul VI, 1968: para. 14).

These conclusions are wide-ranging. They condemn vasectomies,
fallopian tubal ligations, contraceptive sheaths and coils, and contraceptive pills. By insisting that unitive and procreative functions
must never be separated, *in vitro* fertilisation is also disallowed. Nor
is it entirely clear why sexual intercourse is allowed within a marriage when the woman is post-menopausal.

However, the encyclical does make one important concession:

> If there are reasonable grounds for spacing births, arising from the
> physical or psychological condition of husband or wife, or from external
> circumstances, the Church teaches that then married people may take
> advantage of the natural cycles immanent in the reproductive system
> and use their marriage at precisely those times that are infertile, and in
> this way control birth, a way which does not in the least offend the moral
> principles which we have just explained (Pope Paul VI, 1968: para. 16).

This concession is certainly different from Aquinas. There is here a
deliberate emission of semen with the intention that the generation
of new life should not happen. However, the encyclical insists:

Neither the Church nor her doctrine is inconsistent when she considers it lawful for married people to take advantage of the infertile period but condemns as always unlawful the use of means which directly exclude conception, even when the reasons given for the latter practice are neither trivial nor immoral. In reality, these two cases are completely different. In the former married couples rightly use a facility provided them by nature. In the latter they obstruct the natural development of the generative process (Pope Paul VI, 1968: para. 16).

Nature is crucial here and soon became a matter of considerable dispute among married Catholics. Why are some acts considered 'natural' – for example, using modern technology to measure ovulation patterns in order to avoid pregnancy – while others – such as clipping the vas or a fallopian tube – are not? After all, both acts involve medicalised interventions.

Beyond the specific topic of contraception, wider questions were soon debated within Christian ethics about what is to be considered 'natural' and what is not, and about what the ethical significance of 'natural' really is.

For example, is masturbation 'natural'? It certainly occurs within nature, as does homosexual behaviour, and appears to be ubiquitous among human beings. Similarly, is abortion 'natural'? As mentioned earlier, it does seem that a majority of human conceptions are aborted spontaneously (most before they reach the womb). So, if full human life is thought to exist at conception (rather than, as previously thought, within semen), then it would appear that in 'nature' a majority of human beings are never born. In addition, abortive plants (that grow naturally) have been used by women in cultures that long pre-date modern science.

The fact that something is found in 'nature', for many Christian ethicists today, does not readily answer the question of whether it is right or wrong. If they conclude (following Luther) that nature is thoroughly corrupted by sin, then nature may account for very little in ethical terms. If, in contrast, they conclude that nature, despite sin, still shows evidence of God's creative purposes, they might hesitate to be too dogmatic about sexual practices that do seem to be so ambiguous within 'nature'.

## AN EASTERN ORTHODOX PERSPECTIVE ON MARRIAGE AND DIVORCE

In contrast to the plentiful and binding papal teaching, and to the plentiful but non-binding Anglican and Episcopalian reports, on sexuality and marriage, Eastern Orthodoxy makes few public claims about ethical issues (although its bishops have generally taken a strong stance against abortion – despite Greece having some of the highest levels of abortion in Europe). As a result, its ethical assumptions about marriage need to be inferred, at least in part, from its marriage service. From the latter it turns out to be more permissive on marriage after divorce than either the Catholic Church or (until recently) the Church of England.

**Bishop Kallistos Ware** in his 1991 article 'The Sacrament of Love: The Orthodox Understanding of Marriage and its Breakdown' sets out the following paradox:

> In its teaching on marriage, as at many other points, the Orthodox Church adopts a standpoint that has frequently puzzled Western Christians. We affirm two things that at first sight might be thought inconsistent: marriage is a sacrament, and yet under certain circumstances it may be dissolved. We believe firmly in the sacramental character of the marriage union, but according to the Orthodox view sacramentality does not entail indissolubility. The Church has power to permit a divorce, followed by a second marriage; and also a second divorce, followed by a third marriage. A fourth marriage, however, is entirely forbidden in Orthodox Canon Law, whether after divorce or after the death of the previous spouses (Ware, 1991:79–80).

Ware maintains that, since the 17th century, Eastern Orthodox manuals have invariably included marriage in the list of the seven sacraments: 'The marriage rite, as understood by Orthodoxy, is not a contract or agreement made between the two partners but a blessing conferred by the Church.' In addition, Eastern Orthodoxy since the 4th century has included its distinctive crowning of the couple within its marriage service.

All of this suggests a very high doctrine of marriage. However, there is also a distinctive omission:

> Absent from the Orthodox Service is the central event in the Western
> ceremony, the exchange of formal vows. In the Greek practice the
> couple utter no words of consent and make no explicit promises
> during the course of the service itself, and indeed they are neither of
> them required to say anything at all (Ware, 1991:84).

Ware links this omission to the comparative permissiveness of
Eastern Orthodoxy to a church marriage after divorce. The marriage service comes in two parts: the betrothal and the crowning.
At the betrothal the chief ceremony is the blessing of the rings,
which are placed on the hands of bridegroom and bride and are
then exchanged three times. In the past the crowning was omitted
from a marriage following divorce. Today, however, the crowning
is typically retained in such marriages but penitential prayers are
added between the two parts of the ceremony:

> This makes it clear that the second union, although blessed by the
> Church, can never be exactly the same as the first ... two long peni-
> tential prayers are said, which give to the second marriage service a
> spirit altogether different from that which prevails at a first marriage.
> The first prayer begins: 'O Master, Lord our God ... have mercy on our
> sins, and forgive the transgressions of these your servants, calling
> them to repentance and granting them pardon of their offences and
> purification from their sins ... You know the frailty of human nature.'
> The second prayer speaks of the couple as 'unable to bear the heat
> and burden of the day, and not having the strength to endure the
> burning desires of the flesh', and it quotes St Paul's words, 'It is
> better to marry than to burn' (1 Cor. 7.9) (Ware, 1991:88–89).

Ware points out that, in Eastern Orthodox marriage services, this
understanding of marriage as 'a remedy against sin' (a feature of
Church of England wedding services in the past) is entirely absent
for a first-time marriage but is 'heavily emphasized' in a marriage
after divorce.

Many churches in the West today also struggle with the paradox
of reconciling a belief in the life-long nature of marriage and the
widespread presence of divorce among their active members, among
their clergy and, in some instances, among their leaders or bishops.
Remarkably, church marriage after divorce is even prevalent within

otherwise very conservative denominations such as the American Southern Baptists.

As noted in the Introduction, comparing Mark and Matthew's Gospels on the propriety of divorce, it appears that this paradox was also present in the early Church. In Mark, the earlier Gospel, Jesus says emphatically: 'whoever divorces his wife and marries another commits adultery against her; and if she divorces her husband and marries another, she commits adultery' (10.11). In Matthew's gloss this becomes ambiguous: 'whoever divorces his wife, except for unchastity, and marries another commits adultery.'

Inevitably churches have long argued about what constitutes 'unchastity' and whether Matthew (who knew Mark's Gospel) supersedes Mark here or not. Conservative evangelicals, with a strong commitment to the literal truth of Scripture, have been sharply divided on this issue. They may not be helped by Paul's thoroughly confusing advice (written earlier than either Mark or Matthew):

> To the married I give this command—not I but the Lord—that the wife should not separate from her husband (but if she does separate, let her remain unmarried or else be reconciled to her husband), and that the husband should not divorce his wife. To the rest I say—I and not the Lord—that if any believer has a wife who is an unbeliever, and she consents to live with him, he should not divorce her. And if any woman has a husband who is an unbeliever, and he consents to live with her, she should not divorce him. For the unbelieving husband is made holy through his wife, and the unbelieving wife is made holy through her husband. Otherwise, your children would be unclean, but as it is, they are holy. But if the unbelieving partner separates, let it be so; in such a case the brother or sister is not bound. It is to peace that God has called you (1 Corinthians 7.10–15).

Anglicans as a whole are by no means united on this issue, although, in practice, marriage after divorce now occurs frequently within the Church of England. In the Catholic Church, marriage following annulment – that is, not simply after a civil divorce, but after a formal declaration by the Church that the previous marriage, even when the couple have had children together, did not exist – is also becoming more frequent.

This evidence can, of course, be interpreted in different ways. For some it will signify increasing ethical laxity on the part of modern churches. For others it will be seen as a compassionate and pastorally sensitive response by churches. However interpreted, few denominations today wholly resist a church marriage for those whose previous marriage has been dissolved or annulled.

## CASE-STUDY 5: SAME-SEX MARRIAGE AND A QUAKER VIEW OF SEX

In 1957 a group of Quakers – three psychiatrists, two headmasters, a barrister, a psychologist, a teacher of educationally challenged children, a research zoologist and a marriage guidance counsellor – began to meet. They were responding to 'problems brought by young Quaker students, faced with homosexual difficulties, who came to older Friends for help and guidance'.

Significantly, 1957 was the year that the Wolfenden Report on *Homosexual Practices and Prostitution* was published in Britain, recommending that 'homosexual behaviour between consenting adults in private should no longer be a criminal offence'. It also concluded that 'homosexuality cannot legitimately be regarded as a disease'. The Anglican Canon, V.A. Demant, Regius Professor of Moral and Pastoral Theology at Oxford, was a member of the Wolfenden committee and, significantly, did not dissent from its recommendations or conclusions.

In 1963, after several years of discussion, the Quakers published their widely debated report, *Towards a Quaker View of Sex*. However, it was not until 1967 that homosexual practice in England and Wales was decriminalised. Both the Wolfenden committee and the Quaker group were conscious that they were treading on ice. The men that they interviewed could, at that time, have been sent to prison.

*Towards a Quaker View of Sex* is not a work of professional theology. The authors rely too heavily on secondary sources, reaching, for example, the astonishing conclusion that, before Jeremy Taylor's *Holy Living* in the 17th century, 'for the previous fifteen hundred years almost every writer and leader in the Church, both Catholic and Reformed, regarded sexuality as unavoidably tainted with sin, and the sex-relationship in marriage (apart from procreation) as a licensed outlet for the bestial impulses in man'. As seen already, the first part of this claim might apply to Augustine but not to Aquinas.

Its strength, instead, is pastoral and political. It anticipates a shift in Western culture that many people today simply take for granted:

> Nothing that has come to light in the course of our studies has altered the conviction that came to us when we began to examine the actual experiences of people – the conviction that love cannot be confined to a pattern. The waywardness of love is part of its nature and this is both its glory and its tragedy. If love did not tend to leap every barrier, if it could be tamed, it would not be the tremendous creative power we know it to be and want it to be. So we are concerned with the homosexuals who say to each other 'I love you' in the hopeless and bitter awareness of a hostile criminal code and hypocritical public opinion, and also with the anguish of men and women who know they love one another when marriage is impossible and only suffering can be envisaged (Quaker group, 1964:45).

Today, of course, same-sex marriage for gays and lesbians *is* possible within a growing number of Western countries – but, as yet, within only a very few churches. For Methodists, Presbyterians and Anglicans/Episcopalians the issue of same-sex marriage has proved extremely divisive, with ongoing threats of schism.

For Quakers, same-sex marriage has not been so divisive. The authors of *Towards a Quaker View of Sex* suggest why this is so:

> Morality should be creative. God is primarily Creator, not rule-maker. Quakerism from the beginning rejected the idea of particular observances, rituals or sacrament, and instead regarded the whole of life's activities as potentially sacramental. The Quaker movement arose in a time of spiritual stirring. By rejecting all authority save that of the Holy Spirit and the headship of Christ, its vital witness was to an authority which begins in personal experience, in the encounter of man and God in the human spirit and mind (Quaker group, 1964:46).

Their **personalist approach** here is very similar to that of Joseph Fletcher (outlined in the Introduction). Yet it is unlikely to resonate with other forms of Christian ethics based upon biblical and doctrinal principles. Deep divisions about homosexual practice and same-sex marriage soon emerge once these are discussed.

Instructively, the authors of *Towards a Quaker View of Sex* make no mention of the following three crucial New Testaments texts:

- For this reason God gave them up to degrading passions. Their women exchanged natural intercourse for unnatural, and in the same way also the men, giving up natural intercourse with women, were consumed with passion for one another. Men committed shameless acts with men and received in their own persons the due penalty for their error (Romans 1.26–27).
- Do you not know that wrongdoers will not inherit the kingdom of God? Do not be deceived! Fornicators, idolaters, adulterers, male prostitutes, sodomites (1 Corinthians 6.9).
- fornicators, sodomites, slave-traders, liars, perjurers, and whatever else is contrary to the sound teaching (1 Timothy 1.10).

In his 1996 book, *The Moral Vision of the New Testament*, the distinguished evangelical biblical scholar **Richard B. Hays** writes of these texts:

> The only *paradigms* offered by the New Testament for homosexual behaviour are the emphatically negative and stereotypic sketches in the three Pauline texts ... The New Testament offers no accounts of homosexual Christians, tells no stories of same-sex lovers, ventures no metaphors that place a positive construal on homosexual relations (Hays, 1996:394).

He recognises frankly that there are ethical commands in the Old Testament that are not endorsed within the New Testament (for example, about food and circumcision) and for him are therefore not binding upon Christians. He also supports Matthew's position on divorce, regarding this as a legitimate product of practical 'moral deliberation' within the early Christian community. However, the emphatic command in Leviticus 18.22, 'You shall not lie with a male as with a woman; it is an abomination', *is* endorsed within the New Testament and so, for him, it remains binding upon Christians today.

As a result, on same-sex marriage he is emphatic:

> *Should the church sanction and bless homosexual unions?* No. The church should continue to teach – as it always has – that there are two possible ways for God's human sexual creatures to live well-ordered lives of faithful discipleship: heterosexual marriage and sexual abstinence (Hays, 1996:402).

Opponents of Hays' position here have made a number of points. Some argue that treating Paul's writings as a 'law code' is doing exactly what Paul opposes. For Paul it is faith not law that is important. Others point out that it is Paul and not Jesus within the Gospels who makes claims about homosexual practice. Jesus does make emphatic and demanding claims about loving enemies but none about same-sex intimacy.

A different point that some of Hays' critics make is that he pays more attention to Leviticus 18.22 than to Leviticus 20.13, presumably because the latter commands that: 'If a man lies with a male as with a woman, both of them have committed an abomination; they shall be put to death; their blood is upon them.' Few countries today, apart from Uganda, have followed this command literally by proposing to use capital punishment to eliminate homosexual practice. And, in fairness to Hays, Leviticus 20.13 is not endorsed within the New Testament.

More powerfully, some have argued that the lists in 1 Corinthians 6.9 and 1 Timothy 1.10 suggest that it is fleeting and/or coercive relationships that are being condemned. Nowhere in the New Testament is it ever envisaged that there can be intimate same-sex relationships that are committed, exclusive and life-long. In contrast, within a society that has decriminalised homosexual practice people now know otherwise. This radical social change means, so they argue, that this particular part of New Testament teaching should no longer be used to condemn all homosexual practice.

It is not at all easy to see how such conflicting interpretations of these three New Testament texts can be resolved. Perhaps Christians will simply have to learn to live with their strongly held differences on this issue – just as they have done for centuries on the propriety of warfare.

This debate has also exposed another strong division within Christian ethics, in this instance a doctrinal difference. Opponents of homosexual practice are, understandably, for the most part opposed to same-sex marriage. However, some who support homosexual practice (or, at least, tolerate it) have now also become opponents of same-sex marriage. The latter does seem to be the current position of many bishops within the Church of England (but not of their more liberal counterparts within the Scottish Episcopal Church). It is a position they took in their report *Men and Women in Marriage* and in the House of Lords when opposing same-sex legislation in 2013.

This somewhat asymmetric position is usually argued on the basis of a doctrine of marriage, claiming that marriage properly understood can *only* be between a man and a woman. Proponents sometimes quote Genesis 1.27, 'So God created humankind in his image, in the image of God he created them; male and female he created them', to support this claim. Being male or female is God-given, as is marriage. Same-sex marriage, they argue, is contrary to God's created order.

There is no question that legalised same-sex marriage is, for many countries, a recent innovation. However, many opponents of the Church of England bishops on this issue argue that a binary male-female distinction is too simplistic. Human biology has several variants (not everyone is born with straightforward XX or XY chromosomes or sexual organs) and human culture has even more variants. The case-study in Chapter 7 will return to this point in more detail. For the moment, however, maleness and femaleness are increasingly viewed as spectrums within both nature and, increasingly, within modern culture.

Others have argued that, if marriage is considered to be a blessing (as it is within most churches), why should this blessing be denied to gays and lesbians? Should churches not be encouraging gays and lesbians to make exclusive and life-long vows?

Here too it is not obvious how these strongly held claims can be resolved. The issue of same-sex marriage is likely to divide churches for some years to come.

## FURTHER READING

All of the quotations of the following authors in this chapter can be found in greater detail in Section 5 of my *A Textbook of Christian Ethics*:

Aquinas, Thomas (1975), *Summa Contra Gentiles*, 3.2.122–4 & 126 (London: University of Notre Dame Press, andNew York: Doubleday, trans. Vernon J. Bourke, pp. 142–151 & 155–156).

Ware, Kallistos (1995), *The Orthodox Way* (New York: St Vladimir's Seminary Press). This introduction to Eastern Orthodoxy is accessible.

Ware, Kallistos (1997), *The Orthodox Church* (London: Penguin). This introduction to Eastern Orthodoxy is accessible.

## REFERENCES

Faith and Order Commission (2013), 'Men and Women in Marriage': published with the agreement of the House of Bishops and approved for study (London: Church House Publishing). This is accessible and can be found online at: https://www.churchofengland.org/sites/default/files/2017-10/marriagetextbrochureprint.pdf

Hays, Richard B. (1996), *The Moral Vision of the New Testament* (Edinburgh: T&T Clark). Advanced level.

Pope Paul VI (1968), *Humanae Vitae*, available online at: http://w2.vatican.va/content/paul-vi/en/encyclicals/documents/hf_p-vi_enc_25071968_humanae-vitae.html. Fairly accessible.

Quaker group (1964), in Alastair Heron (ed), *Towards a Quaker View of Sex: An essay by a group of Friends* (London: Friends Home Service Committee, revised version, pp. 43–48 & 50). Available online at: https://paganpressbooks.com/jpl/QUAKER.PDF. Accessible.

Ware, Kallistos (1991), 'The Sacrament of Love: The Orthodox Understanding of Marriage and its Breakdown,' in *The Downside Review* (109:375, pp. 79–89).

# RACE AND GENDER

When preparing the first edition of my *A Textbook of Christian Ethics* in the early 1980s I faced a difficult decision. Should I include an extract from **Martin Luther**'s egregious tract *On the Jews and Their Lies*? It might well offend Christians using the textbook and provide ammunition for secular despisers. And it would hardly commend Luther to a post-Holocaust generation of students.

However, frankness prevailed. The Nazi Holocaust was already having a profound effect upon theology and religious studies. In my view it needed to be faced squarely within Christian ethics as well. Within the sociology of religion, Charles Glock and Rodney Stark's 1966 book *Christian Beliefs and Anti-Semitism* had already reached the following shocking conclusion based upon their extensive data:

> We have searched for a religious basis for anti-Semitism. It was suggested that commitment to traditional Christian ideology predisposed persons to adopt a particularistic conception of religious legitimacy, narrowly to consider their own religious status as the only acceptable faith. These features of Christianity were then linked with historical images of the Jews as apostates from true faith and as the crucifiers of Jesus. Subsequently it was shown that orthodoxy, particularism, and a negative image of the historic Jew, combined with a rejection of values of religious libertarianism, overwhelmingly predicated a hostile religious image of the contemporary Jew (Glock and Stark, 1966:130).

In addition there was already influential theological reflection on Christianity and anti-Semitism in Gregory Baum's *The Jews and the*

*Gospel* (1961) and *Religion and Alienation* (1975), Rosemary Radford Ruether's *Faith and Fratricide* (1974) and Charlotte Klein's *Anti-Judaism in Christian Theology* (1978). It was time, I concluded, for Christian ethics to be frank about Luther's anti-Semitism.

## LUTHER ON THE JEWS

*On the Jews and Their Lies* was written in 1543, three years before Luther's death. By this stage his health was seriously deteriorating and the Catholic Counter-Reformation had already begun. He was surrounded by woes and enemies and became increasingly embittered. There is a very sharp and bitter difference between this tract and *That Jesus Christ Was Born a Jew*, a tract he wrote two decades earlier.

Was it just old age that caused this difference? Possibly. However, in Chapter 3 it was noted that, as a younger man, Luther wrote both the irascible *Against the Robbing and Murderous Hordes of Peasants* and the more eirenic *Whether Soldiers, too, Can be Saved* just a year apart. Evidently he was susceptible to huge mood-swings.

*On the Jews and Their Lies* opens with deeply uncomfortable vitriol:

> I had made up my mind to write no more either about the Jews or against them. But since I learned that these miserable and accursed people do not cease to lure to themselves even us, that is, the Christians, I have published this little book, so that I might be found among those who opposed such poisonous activities of the Jews and who warned the Christians to be on their guard against them.

Luther advises his readers not even to waste time trying to debate with Jews, since 'from their youth they have been so nurtured with venom and rancor against our Lord that there is no hope until they reach the point where their misery finally makes them pliable and they are forced to confess that the Messiah has come, and that he is our Jesus'. He depicts Jews as 'crass', 'venomous', 'embittered', 'blind', 'proud', 'raving' and 'stupid' – epithets that would be readily identified today as thoroughly anti-Semitic.

Yet, ironically, he accuses Jews of being the racists:

> There is one thing about which they boast and pride themselves
> beyond measure, and that is their descent from the foremost people
> on earth, from Abraham, Sarah, Isaac, Rebekah, Jacob, and from the
> twelve patriarchs, and thus from the holy people of Israel ... They
> boast of being the noblest, yes, the only noble people on earth. In
> comparison with them and in their eyes we Gentiles (*Goyim*) are not
> human; in fact we hardly deserve to be considered poor worms by
> them. For we are not of that high and noble blood, lineage, birth, and
> descent. This is their argument, and indeed I think it is the greatest
> and strongest reason for their pride and boasting.

He concludes bitterly that, 'I hold that if their Messiah, for whom
they hope, should come and do away with their boast and its
basis they would crucify and blaspheme him seven times worse
than they did our Messiah'.

Even some of Luther's colleagues at the time were shocked by
this savage tract. It is difficult not to see some link between this
tract and the Nazi Holocaust 400 years later.

Of course, this link can be made too simplistically. The expulsion
of Jews and Muslims from Catholic Spain and Portugal in the 1490s
obviously owes nothing to Luther or to Reformed Christianity.
Anti-Semitism is embedded in the medieval Catholic statues of a
number of European cathedrals. Historic Catholic anti-Semitism is
mapped at length by Charlotte Klein. Even Aquinas argued in
favour of segregating Jews within Christian countries. And Muslims
in Iberia in medieval times were equally prone to expelling, and
discriminating against, Catholics. Ancient churches forcibly turned
into mosques and then turned back into churches abound in
southern Spain today.

The distinguished church historian Gordon Rupp, in his 1972
booklet *Martin Luther and the Jews*, concludes judiciously:

> As we follow Luther through the years, we find a signal instance of
> how we become like what we hate. We see a growing obstinacy, a
> hardening of heart, a withering of compassion, a proneness to con-
> temptuous abuse – the very things he thought were the marks of
> judgment on the Jews ... What if not pure doctrine, but suffering be a
> hallmark of the People of God? And if, as Luther thought, Jew and
> Gentile may be bound together in a solidarity of guilt, have we

> perhaps begun to understand what is the greater solidarity of pro-
> mise? May not Jew and Christian together explore this more excellent
> way, in penitence and compassion (Rupp, 1972:22).

Within Christian theology today there is now a widespread
recognition that anti-Semitism tainted some church leaders in the
past and must be carefully avoided in the future.

**The World Council of Churches** (WCC) in the 1960s and
1970s became a focus for Christian opposition to racism in any
form (including anti-Semitism). It had a particularly significant role
in combating apartheid in South Africa, adding pressure for the
release of Nelson Mandela in 1990 and the repeal of apartheid
legislation the following year.

The WCC Uppsala Assembly of 1968 declared that: 'Contemporary racism robs all human rights of their meaning, and is
an imminent danger to world peace.' The Central Committee
meeting at Canterbury in 1969 set out the four aims of its
**Programme to Combat Racism**: '(a) to mobilize the churches in the world-wide struggle against racism; (b) to express in
word and deed solidarity with the racially oppressed; (c) to aid the
churches in educating their members for racial justice; (d) to facil-
itate the transfer of resources, human and material, for projects and
programmes in the field of racial justice.'

By the mid-1970s the Programme to Combat Racism was being
sharply criticised, especially by South African churches that sup-
ported apartheid and by those opposed to **liberation theology**.
The WCC's 1975 document 'Racism in Theology – Theology
Against Racism' defends the programme and criticises churches at
the time for being too inactive in combating racism:

> The evil of racism discloses in a new way how often the churches fail
> to centre around the suffering, dispossessed and degraded members
> of humanity. The churches are constantly yielding to the temptation
> to forget those who are forgotten and not heed the voice of the voi-
> celess. They seek to organize and establish themselves along the lines
> of the main values and dominant forces in their respective societies.
> In varying degrees the histories of our churches bear witness to their
> constant drifting away from the poor and powerless to the rich and
> mighty. The persecutions of defenceless minorities, the ghettos of

Jews in Europe and the recurrent pogroms, the endless stream of refugees, who for the sake of their faith have had to leave their homes and lands – all these have through many centuries left a stain on the history of Christianity (World Council of Churches, 1975).

The authors of this document then challenge churches to 'discipline' their members who are racists, understanding discipline to be 'a consistent effort to help each other to share constructively and hopefully in the suffering that is the result of sin':

The disciplined life in the sacraments and the worship of God provokes rigorous prophetic preaching. Unrepentant racists need to be exhorted that for the health of their souls they are not welcome at the Lord's table until they truly repent. The leadership of the Church needs to be vigorous enough to eradicate preaching and teaching which conforms to personal and institutional racism, and to support preachers and teachers who work against racism. For indifference to racism in the Church is indifference to the worship and service of God (World Council of Churches, 1975).

They call for extensive education on, and against, 'personal and institutional' racism and conclude with a vision of the Christian sacramental community as it should be:

The quality of the discipline of the healing sacramental community of Christians will therefore be determined, particularly at the local level, by the sharing love, pastoral concern and prophetic solidarity in suffering which refuse to leave brothers and sisters to stand alone. The Church must enfold them in its protective arms, encourage, correct and sustain them to return to and persist in the battle against racism (World Council of Churches, 1975).

Set in the context of recent Palestinian history, the feminist theologian **Rosemary Radford Ruether** argues that combating racism sometimes reveals deep internal tensions. She expresses this polemically in the 1992 collection *Faith and the Intifada: Palestinian Christian Voices* that she edited jointly with two liberation theologians, Naim S. Ateek, a Palestinian Anglican, and Marc H. Ellis, a Jewish pro-Palestinian:

One of the most shocking and puzzling phenomena for Middle Eastern Christians is the behavior of Western Christians toward them. Far
from showing concern about the sufferings of Palestinian Christians,
as part of the Palestinian people, Western Christians ignore them, as
if they don't exist. They rush to Israel to see ancient sites of the
Hebrew and Christian Bible, but seem oblivious to the 'living stones'
of those descendants of ancient Christians in the Holy Land. Even
worse, they add their own biblical and theological arguments to support the Zionist takeover of the land of the Palestinians and the
oppression or expulsion of the Palestinian people (Ruether, 1992:147).

The details of Ruether's critique of Christian millennialist evangelicals who support Zionism are not particularly relevant here.
But the central point that she attempts to make is both relevant
and highly contentious:

Appeal to the Holocaust threads through all the other arguments for
Christian support of Israel as well. In each case, any doubt or ques-
tioning of Israel's right to the promised land, that the founding of
that state is a fulfillment of biblical prophecy and a redemptive event
and that Jewish nationalism is an integral part of Judaism is immediately ascribed to Christian anti-Judaism or anti-Semitism. Thus it is
suggested that if Christians doubt any of these propositions, they are
still in the grip of an unreconstructed anti-Judaism. It is this very anti-
Judaism which was the root of the Holocaust. To be critical of Israel
is to be still unrepentantly guilty of the Holocaust (Ruether, 1992:150).

In short, when does criticism of Israel's policies towards Palestinians
become anti-Semitism? For post-Holocaust Western Christian ethicists this is an especially difficult question. Post-colonial Christian
ethicists have faced a similar problem when they contemplate
criticising the current policies of former colonies.

There is widespread consensus among Christian ethicists today
that racism is obviously wrong. Yet atrocities from the past, in
which Christians have been implicated, may still cause tensions
within this consensus. Not the least of the problems here is the
issue of whether or not it is the duty of Christians today to apol-
ogise, or even repent, for the sins of their ancestors. Some conclude that apologies and repentance are appropriate only for

perpetrators to make. **Post-colonial** and **womanist** Christian ethicists, in contrast, often argue that, since Western Christians still benefit economically from the effects of, say, slavery in the past, then they should undertake both repentance *and* restitution to the present-day descendants of African slaves.

## CASE-STUDY 6: DEFINING RACE AND GENDER

There is another tension within this consensus about racism that also affects recent debates about gender. It concerns definitions.

For a while in the 1970s there was a sharp debate about race and IQ. Some at the time argued, controversially, that data on levels of IQ showed that African Americans as a whole scored lower IQ rates than other racial groups. Critics, in contrast, either contested these data and/or the reliability of IQ tests, or they argued that cultural not genetic factors were responsible for the difference. This particular debate has largely abated, but an abiding feature that emerged is that some conclude the very concept of 'race' is largely cultural. Human beings are all human beings who can interbreed across so-called 'races' and who all have mixed genetic inheritances (including varying levels in non-Africans of Neanderthal DNA), as well as having common remote ancestors from Africa.

Even the language still used to denote race – black, white, people of colour, African American, Native American, etc. – is culturally contrived and over-simplifies our mixed genetic inheritances. Such terms are also used for radically different cultural purposes – sometimes to denote personal identity, sometimes to classify relative population balances, and at other times to denigrate people who appear different from ourselves. Recognising this problem, many social surveys today allow respondents to choose for themselves with which category, if any, they wish to identify.

A similar situation is now emerging with gender. For a small percentage of people (the exact number is disputed) there is clear physical evidence of gender diversity, resulting from atypical chromosomes, gonads, phenotypes or hormones. However, there is, in addition, a larger percentage of people who consider themselves to be bisexual or transgender but who do not have any clear physical evidence of gender diversity. As with race, gender for some is now a matter solely of self-declaration.

Christian ethicists have been quite slow to respond to this development. As noted in Chapter 6, defenders of a binary male/female concept of Christian marriage may well resist it strongly. Others, in contrast, may see it as a confirmation, once more, of Galatians 3.28: 'There is no longer Jew or Greek, there is no longer slave or free, there is no longer male and female; for all of you are one in Christ Jesus.' This verse does seem to cover both race and gender (as well as social class), even though Paul would have had no scientific knowledge about physically based gender diversity.

Does it matter that some legal systems now allow people to self-declare their gender without any clear physical evidence? Some argue that it does not, provided that such self-declaration does not involve any harm to others. Others argue that it does matter, even if it does not involve any harm to others, since it distorts God's created order as seen (once again) in Genesis 1.27: 'So God created humankind in his image, in the image of God he created them; male and female he created them.'

Here too these two sides are unlikely to reach a full consensus. Yet they might be able to agree that ethical concerns should be raised if there is evidence that, in some situations, self-declaration is harmful to others. Or, more specifically, if there is evidence that some people might self-declare and then claim **entitlements** that are harmful to others.

This debate has become quite vexed in two particular areas: prisons and competitive sport.

In prisons, trans-women who still have male genitalia might present a real threat to other women prisoners. It is not difficult to see that a predatory male prisoner, who pretends to transition and is transferred to a women's prison, is then likely to have access to some very vulnerable women. Christian **prudence** in this very **personal situation** may well unite those who otherwise disagree about the ethical propriety of gender self-declaration.

Within those sports that favour competitors with greater physical strength or speed, trans-women raise important issues of **justice** towards other female competitors. In addition, these are issues that seldom, if ever, concern trans-men competing with other male competitors.

It may be doubted whether Christian ethicists, who otherwise disagree with each other on the broader issue of gender self-declaration, can offer any specifically Christian resolutions for either of these tricky areas. However, they might at least join with others in seeking resolutions that are **fair** and **compassionate**.

## FURTHER READING

All of the quotations of the following authors in this chapter can be found in greater detail in Section 5 of my *A Textbook of Christian Ethics*:

Baum, Gregory (1975), *Religion and Alienation: A Theological Reading of Sociology* (New York: Paulist Press, 1975).

Luther, Martin (1971), On the Jews and Their Lies in *Luther's Works*, (vol 47, Philadelphia, PA: Fortress Press, trans. Martin H. Bertram, pp. 137–142).

Ruether, Rosemary Radford (1974), *Faith and Fratricide: The Theological Roots of Anti-Semitism* (New York: Seabury Press).

## REFERENCES

Baum, Gregory (1961), *The Jews and the Gospel* (New York: Newman Press). Fairly accessible.

Glock, Charles Y. & Stark, Rodney (1966), *Christian Beliefs and Anti-Semitism* (New York: Harper).

Klein, Charlotte (1978), *Anti-Judaism in Christian Theology* (Philadelphia, PA: Fortress Press). Fairly accessible.

Ruether, Rosemary Radford (1992), in Naim S. Ateek, Marc H. Ellis and Rosemary Radford Ruether (eds), *Faith and the Intifada: Palestinian Christian Voices* (New York: Orbis). Fairly accessible.

Rupp, Gordon (1972), *Martin Luther and the Jews* (London: Council of Christians and Jews). Accessible.

World Council of Churches (1975), 'Racism in Theology – Theology Against Racism.' Faith and Order Commission (Geneva: WCC, Part IV). Accessible.

# THE FUTURE OF CHRISTIAN ETHICS

Viewed in historical terms, the influence of Augustine, Aquinas and Luther upon Western culture has been immense, but each also comes with serious limitations for many people today. Their patriarchy jars badly with modern sensibilities. Luther's attitude towards Jews appals, as does Augustine and Aquinas's acceptance of slavery as part of the natural order.

Nevertheless there are important parts of their separate legacies that endure. Augustine and Aquinas's distinctions between just and unjust wars still have traction with those who reluctantly conclude that armed resistance to defend the vulnerable is sometimes necessary. Luther's single-minded attack upon injustice and hypocrisy still inspires. All three of them wrestled at length with serious social issues that continue to puzzle us today. Each of them was a passionate and dedicated Christian concerned deeply about ethical behaviour.

The previous chapters have attempted to relate modern contributions within Christian ethics to their legacy. Now it is time to move on and to speculate about Christian ethics in the future. What are the challenges that this complex and pluralistic discipline is likely to face in the coming years?

I cannot pretend to have a crystal ball. Who knows what future generations are going to face? The ethical limitations of Augustine, Aquinas and Luther may seem obvious to us now, but our own ethical limitations will doubtless appear just as obvious to our critics in centuries to come. Will they be horrified that we ate mammals? Will they have renounced warfare altogether? Will they continue to value democracy? Will they even be religious?

Instead of guessing, I propose simply to outline some of the existing tensions within Christian ethics that might be explored further: tensions between emerging technology and Christian ethics; tensions between secular humanism and Christian ethics; and tensions between other faith traditions and Christian ethics. In each of these areas there are, I believe, already signs of potentially fruitful dialogue.

## EMERGING TECHNOLOGY AND CHRISTIAN ETHICS

Two highly influential books encouraged many Christian ethicists to regard modern technology with deep suspicion: Jacques Ellul's 1964 book, *The Technological Society*, building upon his shorter 1951 book, *Presence in the Modern World*; and Paul Ramsey's 1970 *Fabricated Man: The Ethics of Genetic Control*.

**Jacques Ellul** (1912–1994) was a Reformed Protestant who was born, lived and died in Bordeaux where, for 36 years, he was Professor of History and the Sociology of Institutions within the faculty of law and economics. The distinguished American sociologist Robert K. Merton introduced *The Technological Society* to an English-speaking audience:

> In Ellul's conception ... life is not happy in a civilization dominated by technique. The technological society requires men to be content with what they are required to like; for those who are not content it provides distractions – escape into absorption with technically dominated media of popular culture and communication ... He has given us a provocative book, in the sense that he has provoked us to re-examine our assumptions and to search out the flaws in his own gloomy forecasts (Ellul, 1964:viii).

Merton's judgment here is soon confirmed by reading *The Technological Society*. Very early in the text Ellul writes:

> But let the machine have its head, and it topples everything that cannot support its enormous weight. Thus everything had to be reconsidered in terms of the machine. And that is precisely the role that technique plays. In all fields it made an inventory of what it could use, of everything that could be brought into line with the machine ...

> Old houses that were not suited to the workers were torn down; and
> the new world technique required was built in their place (Ellul, 1964:5).

A similar sentiment is evident throughout *Presence in the Modern World*:

> The first enormous fact that emerges from our civilization is that
> today everything has become means. The end no longer exists. We no
> longer know where we are heading. We have forgotten our common
> purposes, we have enormous means at our disposal, and we put into
> operation prodigious machines in order to arrive nowhere ... In order
> for the economy to function, human beings must submit to the
> demands of the economic mechanism. As total producers, they place
> all their efforts into the service of production. As obedient con-
> sumers, they swallow blindly all that the economy feeds to them, and
> so on. Thus humanity is transformed into an instrument of these
> modern gods that are our means, and we do it with the good inten-
> tion of making humanity happy (Ellul, 2017:41).

Nor is Ellul cheerful about the prospects for churches in a culture
dominated by machines. He writes about their 'powerlessness' in a
secular world: 'The world in general no longer listens to the
gospel ... Men and women of our day seek other solutions and
heed other promises, other kinds of good news' (2017:92). He
accuses his fellow Christians of hypocrisy and reminds them sharply
of their spiritual responsibility as pilgrims within a world tempted
by the devil. As a Reformed Protestant in Catholic Bordeaux he
did not have a high opinion of the institutional church.

Ellul was also an early critic of the nuclear bombings of Hiroshima
and Nagasaki. In *Presence in the Modern World* he writes:

> In the face of this discovery [of the atomic bomb], this instrument of
> death, humankind retained the possibility of not using it, of not
> accepting this fact. But this question was never even posed. We found
> ourselves before a fact; thus we had to accept it. And from that point
> on, the questions asked were 'secondary'. Who will use this weapon?
> How will its control be arranged? What will be the most expedient: to
> use nuclear power for war, or for peace? How can the economy be
> organized around nuclear power? And so forth, and so on. At no

point was the problem posed of knowing if it was good or evil to embark on this path (Ellul, 2017:23).

Here, for him, is a startling example of a devastating product of technology shaping culture, leading to nuclear proliferation and now to the fearful prospect that some dissident group or nation will once again resort to nuclear warfare.

The fact remains that the only two instances of nuclear bombing were both perpetrated by one of the most democratic countries in the world, but without the knowledge, let alone consent, of its citizens. The pragmatic logic of technology within warfare allowed this to happen: 'Thus human beings divest themselves of their true superiority; and those who claimed to dominate things as well as the world now make themselves slaves of facts, in a way that no dictatorship of the mind had ever dared hope was possible!' (Ellul, 2017:23).

The writings of **Paul Ramsey** (1913–1988) on warfare have already been discussed in Chapter 3. He would almost certainly have dissented from Ellul's critique of the nuclear bombings. However, on emerging techniques in genetics he strikes a very similar note to Ellul. Writing *Fabricated Man* eight years before the birth of the first IVF baby, Ramsey's contacts with medical scientists allowed him to anticipate medical developments that are now standard practice but which he viewed with considerable foreboding.

Although he disagrees with Catholic teaching on contraception, the Methodist Ramsey reaches a very similar position in opposition to IVF:

> In human procreativity out of the depths of human sexual love is prefigured God's own act of creation out of the profound mystery of his love revealed in Christ. To put radically asunder what God joined together in parenthood when He made love procreative, to procreate from beyond the sphere of love (for example … making human life in a test-tube), or to posit acts of sexual love beyond the sphere of responsible procreation (by definition, marriage), means a refusal of the image of God's creation in our own (Ramsey, 1970:38–39).

Unlike Paul VI's *Humanae Vitae* (discussed in Chapter 6) he does not think that every act of sexual intercourse must have both procreative and unitive features. Yet he does believe that the developing technology that soon made IVF possible is wrong wholly to separate these two features:

> To put radically asunder what nature and nature's God joined toge-
> ther in parenthood when he made love procreative, to disregard the
> foundation of the covenant of marriage and the covenant of parent-
> hood in the reality that for a least minimally loving procreation, to
> attempt to soar so high above an eminently human parenthood, is
> inevitably to fall far below – into a vast technological alienation of
> man (Ramsey, 1970:89).

Using language which resonates strongly with Ellul, Ramsey proclaims that: 'men ought not to play God before they learn to be men, and after they have learned to be men they will not play God' (1970:138).

In recent years, however, there are signs of a more nuanced approach to technology emerging within Christian ethics. The Evangelical Brent Waters, the Catholic Lisa Sowle Cahill and the Anglican Elaine Graham, in different ways, provide instructive examples:

**Brent Waters'** two books – his 2006 *From Human to Posthuman: Christian Theology and Technology in a Postmodern World* and his 2014 *Christian Moral Theology in the Emerging Technoculture: From Posthuman Back to Human* – show him increasingly moving away from Ellul.

In *From Human to Posthuman*, Waters was one of the first theologians to explore and challenge the futuristic speculations of Professor Nick Bostrom, Director of the Oxford Future of Humanity Institute, about how technology might so shape human lives that they actually become (and, as Bostrom seems to imply, *should* become) post-human, or even superhuman.

In *Christian Moral Theology in the Emerging Technoculture*, Waters focuses less upon such futuristic speculations and more upon the philosopher Heidegger's bleak assessment of late modernity's technological 'enframement'. Waters distances himself from those who denounce or accept technology as a whole. Instead he argues that Christian worship offers a 'frame' for viewing human living that is not based upon predatory consumption encouraged by technoculture:

The task of Christian moral theology is not merely to condemn pre-datory consumption or scold the nomads of the emerging techno-culture for being thoughtless consumers. Rather, the task is to admit and affirm the necessity of exchange, but to reorient away from pro-moting consumption for its own sake toward enabling communica-tion (Waters, 2014:234).

Returning to **Lisa Sowle Cahill**'s 2003 article 'Bioethics, Theol-ogy and Social Change' (already used in Chapter 6), she gives a very practical example of how Christians can contribute positively to biotechnological intervention:

A striking example from the health care realm is a series of events that in about a two-year period loosened the grip of major pharma-ceutical companies on patented AIDS drugs, making them available cheaply or for free in countries with high rates both of poverty and of AIDS deaths, beginning with South Africa. In this particular example, religious voices, local activism, NGOs, the U.N., market competition from generic drug manufacturers, and market pressure from con-sumers and stockholders all played some part, resulting in a mod-ification of World Trade Organization policy on intellectual property, over which the power of big business had seemed unassailable at the start. Again, the lesson for theological bioethics is that social change is possible even when the entrenched systems of control over goods are infected with structural sin. Forceful intervention can be accom-plished cooperatively, along a spectrum of pressure points, even in the absence of commitment from top-level arbiters of law and policy (Cahill, 2003:385–386).

Cahill contrasts this intervention favourably with the work of individual theologians in the US serving as members of bioethics committees.

But perhaps both roles are important. Despite her pessimism about the secularist turn of bioethics committees, almost two dec-ades later theologians remain members of such committees in the US, the UK and in a number of European countries.

The practical theologian **Elaine Graham**'s 2002 book, *Representations of the post-human: Monsters, Aliens and Others in Popular Culture*, offers another nuanced approach to modern technology. She blends together images of what it is to be human as a result of both changes within science and of changing representations within films and science fiction. Some she finds more enchanting than others.

So she is very conscious that: 'New reproductive technologies, cloning and genetic modification ... promise to engender a future in which the boundaries between humanity, technology and nature will be ever more malleable' (Graham, 2002:3). And she is also aware that popular culture sometimes makes hubristic and fanciful claims about a post-human future – with monsters, cyborgs and invading aliens from outer-space:

> It is a vital task to expose as ideological the appeals to techno-enchant-
> ment, technology making humanity into gods ... The first step will be to
> confound the assumption that transcendence is synonymous with mas-
> tery, disembodied spirituality, fear of contingency and finitude ... Tools,
> artefacts and technologies are extensions and transformations of human
> energies, part of the activity of world-building, not a means of escape
> (Graham, 2002:17).

Her approach is to sift the wheat from the chaff, rather than to oppose technology as whole-heartedly as Jacques Ellul or (in the area of human reproduction) Paul Ramsey. This will surely be an ongoing task for Christian ethicists, since any blanket dismissal of technology soon leads to absurdities.

## EMERGING DIALOGUE BETWEEN SECULAR HUMANISM AND CHRISTIAN ETHICS

The point just made, that theologians remain members of bioethics committees in the US, the UK and in a number of European countries, raises an additional question. How is it that Christian ethicists can and do reach any ethical consensus with secular humanists when their world-views are so different?

For those Christian ethicists convinced by Don Cupitt's 1980 book, *Taking Leave of God*, this is probably not much of a problem. It was seen in Chapter 1 that, ever since that book, Cupitt has adopted a **non-realist approach** to Christian ethics and, indeed, to any form of ethics.

In his 1995 book *Solar Ethics* he states bluntly:

> Solar living ... starts *after* the end of metaphysics and after the
> Death of God, and it is therefore relatively unconcerned about the
> theism/atheism issue. One need not think in such ways. And
> similarly, those who have learnt how to find eternal happiness in
> the purely contingent and outsideless flux of life are delivered from
> the fear of death. It no longer seems in the least unnatural or
> disgusting (Cupitt, 1995:19).

For Cupitt there is no afterlife beyond this world, there is no
ethical objectivity, there is no transcendent God, and Jesus ('the
man') is simply a human prophet:

> Do you see what is emerging? Everything is immanent, everything
> comes down to one level. There is no transcendent moral order, there
> is no inner world within the self, and there is no other sphere of
> action but this common world of ours. There is nothing left for ethics
> to be but that we should love life and pour out our hearts – and that
> is emotivism, or solar ethics. As the man says, 'You are the light of
> the world' (Matthew 5.14). For solar ethics is a version of Christian
> ethics, if one may say so (Cupitt, 1995:9).

So, providing secular humanists can 'love life' and 'pour out' their
hearts, there is little difference between them and Christian ethicists. Or, perhaps more accurately, those Christian ethicists who are
committed to solar ethics differ from secular ethicists only in their
particular attachment to the man Jesus.

As seen earlier, this position is very close to that of Joseph
Fletcher. Yet Fletcher and Cupitt eventually reached very different personal conclusions. Fletcher, towards the end of his life,
self-identified as a secular humanist, whereas Cupitt appears to
remain attracted to a this-worldly form of Christian mysticism:

> Admittedly, the Sun is only a creature. An encounter with God would
> be infinitely more terrible than dropping into a mere twenty-million-
> degree furnace. But in terms of the history of religious symbolism
> death by plunging into the Sun does seem to be a clear metaphor for
> union with God. The mystics have indeed spoken of being consumed

> by fire and of 'dissolving in God' (a Russian phrase). And the meta-
> phor is made all the more attractive by the fact that the Sun's daily
> course across the sky from sunrise to sunset is everywhere seen also
> as a metaphor for human life (Cupitt, 1995:20).

Aquinas recognised more frankly than many other theologians that God-language typically uses manifestly human analogies, symbols or metaphors. In order to depict God, human beings characteristically draw upon terms derived from human experience. Biblical terms such as 'shepherd' or 'king' when applied to God are poetic metaphors (symbols or analogies). God is not regarded as *literally* a shepherd or a king.

So perhaps Cupitt is on firmer ground than some imagine when he explores 'sun' as a poetic metaphor to depict mystical and ethical experience.

Yet, so far at least, he has not convinced most other Christian ethicists to go down such a radically this-worldly poetic path. For them (us) the tension remains between their world-view and that of secular humanists. Can this tension be reduced in a different way?

In their joint 2017 collection, **Religion and Atheism: Beyond the Divide**, the Anglican theologian Anthony Carroll and the philosopher and secular humanist Richard Norman believe that this tension might, indeed, be reduced otherwise:

> Dialogue between believers and atheists, if it is oriented towards
> mutual learning, should help both sides to move beyond their ideol-
> ogies and idolatries. Such dialogue can enable both positions to
> recognise that other options are possible … It can help to temper
> tendencies towards fundamentalisms of both religious and secular
> varieties. It can increase awareness of the complexity and diversity of
> religious and non-religious perspectives, and … correct a misleading
> picture of a simple polar opposition between religion and non-religion
> (Carroll & Norman, 2017:256).

In practice this is what happens within many medical ethics committees at local and national levels. At a local level, in Britain, it is often a hospital chaplain who is a member, or even chair, of the medical ethics committee. Doctors and nurses on such committees will come with a variety of religious and non-religious commitments. At a national level it is typically a professional theologian who is a member, alongside a professional philosopher or bioethicist who, again, might or might not be religious.

At either level such a committee would soon become dysfunctional if believers and atheists were permanently fighting each other. More importantly, if this were to happen it would undermine a central aim of a medical ethics committee – namely to reach an ethical consensus that doctors, nurses and patients alike can adopt, whether they are themselves religious or not. Reaching a consensus that, say, only practising Christians or, alternatively, only committed atheists were able to share would obviously not fulfil this aim.

Within the collection *Religion and Atheism* there is a very striking and fruitful dialogue between former Archbishop of Canterbury Rowan Williams, and the eminent physician, author and humanist Raymond Tallis. This dialogue works so well because, despite their radical differences about whether God exists or whether there is an afterlife, they share a number of stances:

- A suspicion of those who want to reduce everything meaningful to 'scientific explanations'.
- A doubt that eminently free intellectuals can claim convincingly that human free-will is impossible.
- A profound sensibility to language and to metaphors.
- A suspicion of those who claim that ethics is solely about relative emotions.

So, at one point in this dialogue, Tallis says to Williams:

> One of the things that, I feel, you don't think separates us is a set of clearly defined beliefs that can be written down on a piece of paper, and amongst them the idea of God. The reason I'm an atheist and not an agnostic is that any account of the idea of God, to me, always seems to entrain contradictions; and if, as a thinker, I allow self-contradictory notions such as the 'square circle' into the list of things that I believe in or allow, then clearly I may as well give up on thought. But you have already anticipated one anxiety, which is, you set aside the notion of God as a 'thing' within the universe … and you set aside the notion of God as an agent (Carroll & Norman, 2017:4).

Unsurprisingly Williams, in response, nuances both 'thing' and 'agency' using Aquinas's understanding of God-language. Williams is not endorsing Cupitt's non-realism, but he is acknowledging that God-language is not straightforward.

In an article in *Theology*, Tallis goes beyond this point, admitting:

> There is consequently nothing in the secular acknowledgement of our transcendence that can palliate our grief and anguish at our mortality and of those whom we love ... It has to live with the certainty of total extinction. This, moreover, may happen at any time: whoever is born is old enough to die. And it may result from the most trivial of causes. A bang on the head may cancel out all that was brought into being, nurtured, nourished, and cared for by so many of our fellows ... Secular humanism has not only to live with a tragic sense of life and acknowledge that there is no ultimate safety but also that there is no justice or retribution – reward for goodness or punishment for wickedness. Nothing will distinguish the secular afterlife of Hitler from that neither enjoyed nor endured by those who devoted their lives to goodness, or the posthumous fate of tyrants from those whose lives they made living hell. The universe lacks the basis for redemption (Tallis, 2019:122/2).

And then he adds:

> We shall lose the 'organic solidarity' (Durkheim) that comes from the sense of living in the sight of God. In short, the hell feared by some religious believers will be established on earth once the moral capital inherited from religious past has been used up ... The examples of secular religions – ranging from the high ambitions of Comte's Religion of Man to the School for Life with its Sunday services, god-free sermons, and sing-alongs of 'It's a wonderful life' – are not inspiring. There is nothing to reanimate the vision that created the awe-inspiring cathedrals, the spectacular ceremonials, and art of the religion whose spiritual spaces irredentist secularism would wish to reclaim (Tallis, 2019:122/2).

The position that Tallis takes here is certainly not that of militant secularists. He recognises that there is a 'moral capital inherited from religious past' that represents a real loss in the present.

Equally, Rowan Williams recognises the complexities of God-language and the frailties of churches as institutions. At the same time Williams does not follow Cupitt's present assertions: that there is no afterlife beyond this world; that there is no ethical objectivity; that there is no transcendent God; and that Jesus ('the man') is simply a human prophet. Sensitive secular humanists and sensitive Christian ethicists may have something important to learn from each other without each abandoning their deepest commitments.

## EMERGING DIALOGUE BETWEEN CHRISTIAN ETHICS AND OTHER FAITH TRADITIONS

In the Introduction to this book the significance of the emerging discipline of **Abrahamic ethics** was acknowledged – a term derived from the fact that Judaism, Christianity and Islam all recognise Abraham as a key figure (whether as patriarch or prophet). It was noted that there are broad theological beliefs held in common by all three of these faith traditions – especially a belief that the world is created by an all-compassionate God and that life is God-given and endures, in some sense, beyond death.

Clearly a belief in a divine, compassionate Creator is not shared with secular humanists or, indeed, with a substantial number of Buddhists, but it is shared with believers within and beyond these three faith traditions. In a pluralist society Abrahamic ethics might become increasingly significant, especially once it is recognised by more open-minded followers that Judaism, Christianity and Islam face similar challenges today.

Crucially, one of their greatest challenges is that the sacred Scriptures that inspire and shape the lives of their followers also contain texts that appear to encourage violence, racism and patriarchy and are, therefore, deeply offensive to modern sensibilities. Some traditionalists might respond: 'Well that is just too bad – it is modern sensibilities that are the problem.' But, for other followers, 9/11 was a decisive turning point, perpetrated as it was by pious (and educated) men (and no women) holding a deep hatred of Westerners.

At several points in this book the issue of **religiously inspired violence** has been discussed as a very serious problem for Christian ethicists using the Bible. Chapter 7 also discussed the issues of patriarchy and racism, evident at times within the Bible and within Christian tradition. Jewish and Islamic ethicists face similar problems of religiously inspired violence, as the following texts suggest:

> When the Lord your God brings you into the land that you are about to enter and occupy, and he clears away many nations before you— the Hittites, the Girgashites, the Amorites, the Canaanites, the Perizzites, the Hivites, and the Jebusites, seven nations mightier and more numerous than you— and when the Lord your God gives them over to you and you defeat them, then you must utterly destroy them. Make no covenant with them and show them no mercy ... You shall devour all the peoples that the Lord your God is giving over to you, showing them no pity; you shall not serve their gods, for that would be a snare to you ... Moreover, the Lord your God will send the pestilence against them, until even the survivors and the fugitives are destroyed (Deuteronomy 7.1–2, 16 & 20).

> But as for the towns of these peoples that the Lord your God is giving you as an inheritance, you must not let anything that breathes remain alive. You shall annihilate them—the Hittites and the Amorites, the Canaanites and the Perizzites, the Hivites and the Jebusites—just as the Lord your God has commanded, so that they may not teach you to do all the abhorrent things that they do for their gods, and you thus sin against the Lord your God. If you besiege a town for a long time, making war against it in order to take it, you must not destroy its trees by wielding an axe against them. Although you may take food from them, you must not cut them down. Are trees in the field human beings that they should come under siege from you? (Deuteronomy 20.16–19).

> Do not think that I have come to bring peace to the earth; I have not come to bring peace, but a sword.
> For I have come to set a man against his father,
> and a daughter against her mother,
> and a daughter-in-law against her mother-in-law;
> and one's foes will be members of one's own household.
> Whoever loves father or mother more than me is not worthy of me; and whoever loves son or daughter more than me is not worthy of me' (Matthew 10.34-37).

Whenever you encounter the idolaters, kill them, seize them, besiege them, wait for them at every lookout post (Sura 9.5).

Fight those people of the Book who do not [truly] believe in God and the Last Day, who do not forbid what God and His Messenger have forbidden, who do not obey the rule of justice, until they pay the tax and agree to submit (Sura 9.29).

Believers, why, when it is said to you, 'Go and fight in God's way,' do you feel weighed down to the ground? Do you prefer this world to the life to come? How small the enjoyment of this world is, compared with the life to come! If you do not go out and fight, God will punish you severely and put others in your place, but you cannot harm Him in any way: God has power over all things. (Sura 9.38–39).

And the following verses suggest that Christianity and Islam have a similar problem with texts that have inspired **anti-Semitism**:

After this Jesus went about in Galilee. He did not wish to go about in Judea because the Jews were looking for an opportunity to kill him. Now the Jewish festival of Booths was near ... The Jews were looking for him at the festival and saying, 'Where is he?' And there was con- siderable complaining about him among the crowds. While some were saying, 'He is a good man', others were saying, 'No, he is deceiving the crowd.' Yet no one would speak openly about him for fear of the Jews (John 7.12 & 11–13).

[Jesus said:] 'I know that you are descendants of Abraham; yet you look for an opportunity to kill me, because there is no place in you for my word ... You are from your father the devil, and you choose to do your father's desires. He was a murderer from the beginning and does not stand in the truth, because there is no truth in him. When he lies, he speaks according to his own nature, for he is a liar and the father of lies. But because I tell the truth, you do not believe me (John 8.37 & 44–45).

So when Pilate saw that he could do nothing, but rather that a riot was beginning, he took some water and washed his hands before the crowd, saying, 'I am innocent of this man's blood; see to it your- selves.' Then the people as a whole answered, 'His blood be on us and on our children!' (Matthew 27–24.25)

> Says the Prophet: 'You who follow the Jewish faith, if you truly claim that out of all people you alone are friends of God, then you should be hoping for death'. But because of what they have stored up for themselves with their own hands they would never hope for death – God knows the wrongdoers very well (Sura 62.6).

> Those children of Israel who defied [God] were rejected through the words of David, and Jesus, son of Mary, because they disobeyed, they persistently overstepped the limits, they did not forbid each other to do wrong. How vile their deeds were ... God is angry with them and they will remain tormented (Sura 5.78 & 80).

And, on **patriarchy**, these two texts have proved particularly troublesome for modern readers:

> Wives, be subject to your husbands as you are to the Lord. For the husband is the head of the wife just as Christ is the head of the church, the body of which he is the Saviour. Just as the church is subject to Christ, so also wives ought to be, in everything, to their husbands (Ephesians 5.22–24).

> Husbands should take good care of their wives, with [the bounties] God has given to some more than others and with what they spend out of their own money. Righteous wives are devout and guard what God would have them guard in their husband's absence. If you fear high-mindedness from your wives, remind them [of the teaching of God], then ignore them when you go to bed, then hit them (Sura 4.34).

It is easy simply to reject these texts and to focus, instead, upon texts that are considered to be more agreeable (**cherry-picking** again). However, if their possible influence upon behaviour is taken seriously then responsible ethicists might be wise to consult their Jewish, Christian or Muslim colleagues. Perhaps they could learn from each other.

Christian ethicists today typically argue that all of these New Testament texts need to be set into the context of early Christianity. The Ephesians passage can be compared with other contemporary 'household codes' and with other aspects of the household code in Ephesians. They note that in the next chapter of Ephesians there is this command: 'Slaves, obey your earthly masters with fear and trembling, in singleness of heart, as you obey Christ.' It is then sometimes argued (with more than a touch of irony) that, if this particular household code is to be regarded as normative for Christians today, both wives *and* slaves are still required to be obedient.

Similarly, the stark statements about Jews in John and, sometimes, Matthew – and the relative absence of such texts in Mark – are now sometimes set into the historical context of changing relationships between Jews and Christians at the time. In what is often called the Second Temple period, reflected in Mark, these relationships were less antagonistic than they were, within and between Christian and Jewish communities, in the subsequent period.

A number of significant Islamic scholars have pointed out that all of the texts from the Qur'an, just quoted, come from a second and, again, more antagonistic phase of early Islam in relation to other faith groups, when the Prophet moved from Mecca to Medina. In this latter phase followers of the Prophet were themselves being actively persecuted. Understood in this way, some Islamic scholars now argue that these texts represent the frustration of the persecuted rather than a call for a violent *jihad* that is to be emulated today.

Similarly, scholars of the Tanakh (Hebrew Bible) typically set the *herem* texts into their historical context of contesting faith/ethnic groups. Many conclude that the primary concern of *herem* (translated as 'ban') was the purity of worship and community within Israel. This strand within Deuteronomy was deeply concerned with preventing idolatry, believing that idolatry – carried out by the different peoples of Canaan – would bring about the destruction of Israel. From this perspective the annihilation of idolatry was the primary aim of *herem*: the annihilation of the peoples of Canaan was a means to this end but not its primary aim. The Greek rather than Hebrew version of Deuteronomy (New Testament writers tended to use this Greek version) brings this out more clearly – sometimes using a word meaning 'curse' rather than 'annihilate' – as does the occasional use of *herem* elsewhere in the Tanakh simply for sacrificial animals 'devoted' to God (e.g., Leviticus 26.29) and the use in Arabic of *harim* for a household space devoted for women.

As noted in Chapter 3, the great medieval Jewish scholar Maimonides concluded that, in context, *herem* applied to Canaanites was not to be considered an abiding command. In addition, historians today tend to view it as an aspiration of this strand within Deuteronomy and not a depiction of actual practice, and few if any Jewish scholars today regard it as an excuse for genocide.

By learning from each other about how to understand difficult texts within their respective Scriptures, Jewish, Christian and Islamic ethicists may also learn how to cooperate on some of the most pressing global issues facing us today. If climate change, in particular, is to be addressed effectively, then (as seen in Chapter 4) a global change in human behaviour will be needed. No single faith tradition can, on its own, bring about that change. It requires cooperation across faith traditions.

As mentioned earlier, there are broad doctrines and values held in common by all three of these faith traditions. Without agreeing, say, about the divine status of Jesus, they might yet agree upon some of the values that Jesus shared with Judaism and that are also enshrined within the Qur'an – such as the values of compassion, care, faith/trust and humility mentioned in the Introduction – and it is values like these that can enrich public discourse *and* be shared by some secular and religious humanists alike.

The emerging dialogue within **Abrahamic ethics** is, I believe, a precious sign of hope for a better future.

## FURTHER READING

Cahill, Lisa Sowle (2004), *Bioethics and the Common Good* (Milwaukee, WI: Marquette University Press). Advanced.

Cahill, Lisa Sowle (2005), *Theological Bioethics* (Washington, DC: Georgetown University Press).

## REFERENCES

Cahill, Lisa Sowle (2003), 'Bioethics, Theology and Social Change,' in *Journal of Religious Ethics* (31:3, pp. 366–371, 378–379 & 385–386).

Carroll, Anthony & Norman, Richard (eds) (2017), *Religion and Atheism: Beyond the Divide* (London: Routledge). Mostly at an advanced level.

Cupitt, Don (1995), *Solar Ethics* (London: SCM Press) and *Taking Leave of God* (London: SCM Press, 1980). Accessible.

Ellul, Jacques (1964), *The Technological Society* (Toronto: Vintage Books). Generally accessible.

Ellul, Jacques (2017), *Presence in the Modern World* (originally written in French in 1948, first published in English in 1951, and in a new translation, used here, by Lisa Richmond, Cambridge: James Clark). Generally accessible.

Graham, Elaine (2002), *Representations of the post-human: Monsters, Aliens and Others in Popular Culture* (Manchester: Manchester University Press, and New Brunswick, NJ: Rutgers University Press). Advanced level.

Pope Paul VI (1970), *Humanae Vitae* (London: Catholic Truth Society, revised edition). Fairly accessible and can also be found online at: http://w2.vatica n.va/content/paul-vi/en/encyclicals/documents/hf_p-vi_enc_25071968_ humanae-vitae.html

Ramsey, Paul (1970), *Fabricated Man: The Ethics of Genetic Control* (New Haven, CT: Yale University Press). See also References in Chapter 3 for Ramsey's other books. Fairly accessible.

Tallis, Raymond (2019), 'Human transcendence: the possibility of spiritual irredentism,' in *Theology* (Vol. 122, No. 2, March) and 'Science, stories and the self: A conversation between Raymond Tallis and Rowan Williams,' in Anthony Carroll and Richard Norman (eds), *Religion and Atheism: Beyond the Divide* (London: Routledge, 2017, pp. 3–23). Accessible.

Waters, Brent (2014), *Christian Moral Theology in the Emerging Technoculture: From Posthuman Back to Human* (Farnham, UK, and Burlington, VT: Ashgate) and *From Human to Posthuman: Christian Theology and Technology in a Postmodern World* (Farnham, UK, and Burlington, VT: Ashgate, 2006). Advanced level.

Williams, Rowan (2017), 'Science, stories and the self: A conversation between Raymond Tallis and Rowan Williams,' in Anthony Carroll and Richard Norman (eds), *Religion and Atheism: Beyond the Divide* (London: Routledge, pp. 3–23). Accessible.

Quotations from the Qur'an come from M.A.S Abdel Haleem's translation (Oxford: Oxford World's Classics, 2008).

# INDEX

Printed in the United States
by Baker & Taylor Publisher Services